My Korean Identity and Quest for Understanding

Essays by Korean Youth around the World

Korean Youth Studies

Number 1

My Korean Identity and Quest for Understanding

Essays by Korean Youth around the World

Edited by
Sora Yang

KOREANI

Edison * Seoul * Bangalore * Cebu

My Korean Identity and Quest for Understanding: Essays by Korean Youth around the World (Korean Youth Studies, 1)

Copyright ©2008 KOREANI

Hardcover ISBN13: 978-1-59689-062-6
Paperback ISBN13: 978-1-59689-147-0

Write To Address:
Koreani Press
P. O. Box 756
Edison, New Jersey 08818-0756
The United States of America

The United States of America
Library of Congress Control Number: 2008941353

Dedicated to Korean youth all over the word
From Australia to India to Africa to the USA
And everywhere else in the world
Who seek to empower themselves
And make the world a better place

Table of Contents

Table of Contents

Korean Youth Studies

Korean Youth Studies is a literary and intellectual effort launched by Koreani Press to preserve oral history of ethnically Korean youth from around the world. Although the majority of Koreans live in South Korea and North Korea, currently, there are growing communities throughout the world.

China has the largest ethnically Korean population, estimated to be well over 3 million ethnic Koreans, outside of the Korean peninsula. The country with the second largest ethnically Korean population outside of the Korean peninsula is the United States of America, with an ethnic Korean population a little bit over 2 million. Both Korean communities are growing in China and the United States.

Besides China and the USA, large ethnically Korean populations can be found in Russia, Kazakhstan, Brazil, Argentina, Canada, Australia, New Zealand, Great Britain, Germany, and France, to name a few countries.

Each country has a well-organized Korean Community Center (KCC) and a plethora of Korean churches. Each country tends to have an Ecumenical Korean Churches Council for that nation and/or continent. Korean churches tend to be evangelical in faith and reformed/Calvinist in theology.

In some sense, Korean churches play a more important role than Korean Community Centers (KCC) for the Koreans of any country outside of Korea. Many Koreans are proud that Korea sends the second largest number of Christian missionaries around the world after the United States of America.

In the United States of America, the leader (Chairman of the Board of Directors) of the Ecumenical Korean Churches Council of the United States of America, comprising nearly 100% of the Protestant Korean denominations (and Korean presbyteries, synods, conferences, etc. belonging to American denominations, mainline and evangelical) is Rev. Manwoo A. Kim of the First Korean Presbyterian Church of Philadelphia (2008-2009 Term, voted in by unanimous decision).

Korean youth who have contributed to this volume have all distinguished themselves in some way as future leaders of the Korean community. Those whose article was included here had to undergo a rigorous review process, including by renowned Korean academics. They are all recognized by their own local Korean community leaders as future leaders who will make Koreans shine. They have the support of the Korean communities to which they belong and the endorsement of Korean governing bodies.

Their story is the story of Every-Korean. Their testimony is the evidence of the vibrancy of the Korean population throughout the world. Their dedication is the dedication to empower the Korean people.

Korean Youth Studies, therefore, is a socio-historical publication series of highest import. The first volume, *My Korean Identity and Quest for Understanding*, provides important sociological and historical resource for academics and scholars in the field of Korean studies, Asian-American Studies, Ethnic Studies, Anthropology, Sociology, Social Work, and Communications.

Furthermore, the first volume of the Korean Youth Studies series helps those who want to understand Korean youth better with accurate information and testimonies by those who are a part of the living experience of Korean communities around the world.

And this book helps Korean youth globally who are in search of their own identity as Koreans living in foreign lands.

"A Girl Down Under"[1]

Sora Yang (Baulkham Hills Selective High School, AUSTRALIA)

---

[1] This is the 1st place essay for the 2008 Global Rev. Ham Suk-Hyun Essay Contest on the topic of "My Korean Identity."

"A Girl Down Under"

I'm a sixteen year old girl. Like a lot of you out there, an ordinary teenager.

I'm now in my junior year of high school, sometimes temporarily stressed out – but I always recover (almost) completely sane.

I like to read, go shopping, listen to music, and talk with friends.

Appearance? Average height, average weight, average looks – nothing traffic-stopping.

Just your everyday girl.

A girl who happens to be Korean.

I live in the land of down under; yes, where the kangaroos bounce around in the bush, and koalas sleep in trees. I live on the biggest island in the world, or the smallest continent - with a comparatively tiny population of 21 million, living on almost 8 hundred thousand km. I live in a country that was originally a destination for convicts from England, now an amazing patchwork of a country, made of people from all over the world. I'm part of one of those patches that make up Australia –
I'm an ordinary Korean teenager living in a predominantly Caucasian country.

I've lived in Australia for 15 years now, as far as I can remember. I was one and a half when my parents brought me out here from Daejeon, Korea. We've always lived in Sydney – first in a flat in Meadowbank, then Epping, Carlingford, and finally, our own house in Beecroft, adding new family members along the way. For all intents and purposes, I guess I'm categorized as an Australian – I just happen to have a Korean passport.

Aussie Aussie Aussie, Oi Oi Oi? Or 대~한민국, clapclap-clapclap-clap?

2

Korean? Australian? One or the other? Is it either or both? *Who* am I? *What* am I? *Where* am I from? These were always vague, ever present thoughts rolling around at the back of my head. On the surface, nothing showed – I was caught up in the complicated and dizzying ride that was growing up. You're not even 50% sure of anything, all you can do is go onwards – stumbling, staggering, falling over. Forward.

Everyone out there, you agree, growing up can be hard? School, Friends, Family. Everything just seems to get complicated simultaneously. Throw in cultural identity, and what do you get?

You tell me.

I'm a lucky person, a lucky sixteen-year old girl. But growing up is hard, as it was for me, and may be, for everyone. Don't get me wrong; we're all awesomely blessed in being able to live in countries without war, poverty, disease – but it doesn't change the fact that it is somewhat overwhelming to live in a country where most people don't look anything like you, or go to a school where nobody talks like you. Australia (more specifically, in my case, Sydney), in general terms, is a wonderful place to live in. I suppose we ought to have a version of the concept of the 'American Dream' for Australia. But like John Meynard Keynes said "When the facts change, I change my mind," and depending on the situation, reality mightn't be as rosy as expected.
As it was the case for me.

Let me tell you a true story, about a little girl moving to a new school, and what happened after.

The curtain opens.

Act 1, Scene 1.
Once there was a little girl, with black hair, brown eyes, and a rather flat nose. One day, she moved to a new school where nobody looked much like her. She was a novelty; at the time – the new girl that everyone wanted to introduce to the school – everyone volunteered to be her 'buddy'. In the end, two girls in year 2 were chosen, and led they her proudly around the school.

"A GIRL DOWN UNDER"

She was happy. Everyone fell over their feet being nice to her, and things were just peachy.
For a while.

Act 2, Scene 1. *It's the year 2000. The little girl is in year 3.*
It's a new school year, and she is eager to start school. All the children file in to the assembly hall, to be allocated to their new classes. One by one the names are called out, she waits; her name is at the very end. There go her friends – look, they're all in the same class.
And at last – her name is called out.
But fate has some fun - say goodbye to your playmates, little girl, it's a different class for you.
The year of the Sydney Olympics will be a memorable year.
This is the year of the conception of the 'We Hate So Ra' Club.
The little girl's name is So Ra.

Act 2, Scene 2. *It's still year 2000.*
Kids are grouped off in little cliques, in the playground, under leafy trees, on the asphalt.
Look in the corner over there. Three little girls laughing over something.
A fourth girl approaches hesitantly. The three girls turn away, huddling closer together, lowering their voices.
The fourth little girl looks unsure of herself, hovering on the edges of the little group.
The 'We Hate So Ra' Club is thriving.
The novelty's worn off.
So Ra is a number four, a lost little waif in the playground.

Act 2, Scene 3.
The court lines on the asphalt have been re-painted, and the trees are indiscernibly bigger.
It's a change from silent discussions with Sky and Clouds -
Girl number four reads a book on the cement stairs, in an empty corner of the playground.
Another book to add her list of 'to-reads', half the titles lost in the seemingly infinite progression of titles.
Another lunchtime whiled away with books and the company of Solitude.

4

Act 3, Scene 1.
The "We Hate So Ra" Club disbanded after two years.
An anonymous bystander had told the teacher about the club.
The teacher was furious, and stamped on the flame.
So Ra didn't know who it was, but she was grateful, in a distant way.
She was used to the many lunchtimes with Solitude, and the occasionally present Spite.
The 'We Hate So Ra' Club flickered for a while, and died out.

Two years is a long time, but as all good things come to an end, so does the bad.
So Ra was 10 years old.

I am So Ra.

Minus the space between the two syllables, and swap the R for an r.
I'm now Sora to the English-speaking population.
My new and improved name.
Why the mini-makeover? The reason is kind of funny, really. See, when teachers marked the class attendance list, they'd get to my name, and call out *part* of my name:
"umm.. So? So? So Yang?"
Girl number four puts her hand up midst the giggles and catcalling, and corrects the teacher patiently.
So What? No, it's So **Ra**, thank you very much.

It was a little thing, but little things pile up. Not having a name like Sarah, Jane or Mary... The incessant jokes about my name, and of course, the way I looked. Flat-set eyes, a comparatively flat nose – the jokes wear thin after a while, and start to cut. Again and again. I would laugh it off, but inside, I was bleeding. Did it matter that I looked different from everyone else? So I didn't have deep set eyes, a pointy nose, fair skin, non-black hair, like almost everybody else. So what?
It's not my fault. 'It's what's inside that counts' isn't it?'
Let me be.
I was confused, I was hurt.
I couldn't understand why those kids hated me, enough to start a 'We Hate So Ra' Club.

5

Maybe I was just a little different – I looked different, I could talk different.
But of course I was different, weren't we all different?
Isn't that what makes us special?
Treat me the way you would want to be treated.
Please.

Bullying is a horrible thing, and I'm sure that everyone gets bullied some time in their life. Why? I don't know. I don't think those kids that bullied me were being racist. I think that people get bullied because they don't completely belong. I suppose that I didn't belong, not 100%. I wasn't part of "the hidden language of laughter and silliness... that was, somehow, friendship" (*Keeping the Moon* by Sarah Dessen). It's hard to explain if you haven't experienced it yourself, but everyone else seems to hold a sort of grudge against you, about something you can't quite put your finger on, but it's there all the same. Because to belong, generally, you have similarities with your group, if not that, it's your friendship that holds you together, the friendship that realizes and accepts the differences and flaws as part of who you are – you're taken in lock, stock and barrel. But I wasn't. I wasn't someone they could relate to, nor was I a completely accepted friend.

Belonging. In retrospect, I realize, I felt lost. I was a misfit, neither here nor there. Not completely Australian, not completely Korean. I think this was the reason for the distance I felt from my schoolmates – I wasn't completely one of *them* – I wasn't absorbed into their way of life. Yes, I spoke English, but I also spoke Korean. Yes, I ate sandwiches, but I also ate rice and kimchi. I was a puzzle piece that was trying to fit into a certain place, but my edges didn't conform to the gaps left by the other puzzle pieces. I didn't see things in the same way as everyone else, I didn't quite 'get' some things – the answer to the rhetorical 'you know what I mean?' was always a no. Laughing a second too late at a joke I didn't quite understand, having nothing to contribute to the "what was on TV last night" discussion, looking blankly back at a person who's trying to explain why something's the way it is (for them).
  "What's your team?" - What team? [He meant the AFL teams.]

SORA YANG

"Who do you think's gonna end up leaving?" - Who? What? [She meant the latest conflict that was happening on an episode of 'Home and Away' the night before.]
Little things that add up.

So what happened in those two years of the 'We Hate So Ra' Club? How did I cope? What did I do? Pretty much what you'd expect, really. I went to library and read books; I was the librarian's favourite little bookworm, I was a library monitor in year 5 and 6 – my library record of books read in one year was 482. The librarian was a cheerful woman, I think she had white hair, but she wasn't really that old. I don't know whether she knew about my lack of playmates, but I remember she'd always talk to me when I went to borrow my books, chatting about the weather and making small talk. Ours was a small school, and the library was tiny – just two adjoined rooms with a small office in the middle, but even so, I never did manage to read all the books in the library. I did read most of them, though. Favourite books? Books that were favourites at the time, were *A Little Princess* by Frances Hodgson Burnett, and *The Little White Horse* by Elizabeth Goudge. Another book, one my mother had bought for me from a second hand store (sometimes they sell really good books cheap) was *Gone with the Wind* by Margaret Mitchell, still a favourite of mine. Yes, you've noticed, they all have young heroines? I suppose, subconsciously, I liked the idea of other girls overcoming adversity, whatever form of it, to emerge more or less triumphant. Books were my refuge, my way of not hiding from, but rather coping with reality.

What else was there? I threw myself into studying – being the best academically was the only edge I claimed. Here, I owe it all to my mother: weekdays, after school I would come home, and she would sit with me for minimum of two hours, working through the textbooks she'd bought for me. I remember that I couldn't remember my multiplication tables properly, so she made a tape with a recording of herself reading out the multiplication tables from one to twelve. She sounded so tired on the tape, sometimes I cried while listening to her voice, memorizing the tables. I felt that I had to do well, for the sake of my mother, as well as for myself.
I know them now, front to back, back to front.

7

"A Girl Down Under"

I came equal first in the Mathematics Olympiad, along with two other students, two Caucasian boys.
It felt good to be first.

I got used to doing well, but it wasn't enough. Yes, I suppose I was greedy, but I craved to be the best. Second or third, 'exceeds expectations,' wasn't good enough. I had to be first, or nothing. At the time, I suppose my self-worth was dependent on my academic performance. It's not a very healthy place to be in, but it pulled me through. To me, whatever happened to me, whatever people said or did, didn't matter – I was secure in the confidence that I was better than them academically, I could beat them.

Besides school on weekdays, I went to school on Saturdays too – Korean School. It was just another difference between me and my schoolmates. When they went out to play sports, meet up, I was slaving away at Korean School. It was hard, because even here, I didn't fit in. All the kids were short term students from Korea, they were pretty much 100% Korean. I never shined academically there; I couldn't catch up to those kids – we used textbooks made for Korean students in Korea. I was always, always behind, and I would beg my mother to let me stay at home. But my mother was resolute, and off I went, every Saturday, the tortoise that plodded along behind the effortlessly sprinting hares.

To make up for my lack of extra-curricular activities, in year 5 and 6, I joined the debating club. All the debates, meetings, practice sessions blur into a mess; the only clear debate I remember was the finals in year 5, which we won. In general, I wasn't one of the speakers all the time – I had, and still have, the tendency to speak quickly, too quickly, for a lot of people to understand. But it was great fun, being part of a team, winning together, losing together, discussing tactics and strategy together.

Honestly, I don't really remember much about my primary school years – the bullies were a minority. The fact that there was a "We Hate So Ra" Club is a stain on my vague memories. So I was bullied in primary school, sometimes outright hostility, usually the kind of subtle exclusion and snide comments that's hard to pinpoint; the seeming friendliness turning to sudden coldness at the drop of a hat, back and forth like a weathervane. Yes, I was teased and ostracized by a few, and spent lunchtimes alone. I know that it was hard at the time, but I was a little girl, and fortunately, resilient, with supportive and reassuring parents who assured me that it would all blow over in time, and to ignore the bullying. I took it to heart, and tried not to be much bothered by the exclusion. And it turned out to be true, didn't it? I'm fine now. Primary school wasn't so bad.

Act 4, Scene 1. The presentation evening, the little girl is graduating from primary school.
She sits on her chair, as all the other names are called out, for different awards.
One by one, they all leave.
Solitude returns for a kiss goodbye.
There is only one award left.
Walking across the stage, she knows everyone is looking at her, her classmates, teachers, parents.
Everyone.
Victory is sweet, an almost tangible taste she can feel at the back of her throat, mixed with excitement, it's intoxicating.
She is set apart, special.
Girl number four is Dux.

High school was a whole new place altogether. It was a chance for me to start again; as cliché as that sounds, it was true – I was the only person from my school here, nobody knew me, or what had happened to me. See, I attended a "selective" school – students have to sit a statewide exam, and apply for the school they want to attend. Depending on the rank of the school, you have to get a certain mark to be accepted. These selective schools are mostly made up of Asian students; generally the higher ranked the school, the more Asian students there are. Most kids go to coaching college from year 3 to start preparing for these exams, to sit the exam in year 6. I studied with my mother at home, and I got into one of the best high schools in the state. At least 90% of the students were Asian. Maybe it was because parents wanted something better for their children, because they pushed their kids to study-study-study hard for the entrance exam. This might be a generalization, but from where I stand, it seems that Asians are more motivated and academically superior to

Australian-born Caucasian counterparts, simply because we put more effort into our studies. It's different for Anglo-Saxon people – they're secure in knowing they belong to this country – their ancestors might have been convicts who worked the land to make it become what it is now. Because they've been part of this culture since before they can remember, they've literally been born and bred Australian. But as immigrants, we have to make our own place.

Here, at high school, I could relate to my schoolmates. They ate the similar foods as me, they looked like me, they had the same kind of parents – well-meaning, but sometimes unbearably pushy in their determination to make us the very best of the best. In most cases, there were a never-ending line of tutors, coaching college classes, music lessons. Behind it all, the constant expectation to do well, and the nagging feeling, even responsibility to have to do well, the dread of failure. That's how it felt to us, anyway. And so there I was – a high school student.

For me, Year 10 was the year that everything fell into place. It was the year that I read the first book that made me cry. A Korean book, incidentally, in Korean – 가시고기, phonetically "gashigogi," meaning "spined stickleback," a sort of fish. Plot-wise, it was a fairly simple book, but the emotional undertones and contextual themes were what stood out. It's a story about a father (a poet) and his son (academically and artistically gifted). The little boy is sick with leukemia, and knows he's dying, but doesn't tell his father that he knows. In the end, ironically, it is the father that dies, after selling off his eye to pay for his son's medical fees, while writing a book of poetry to publish. The boy lives, and leaves for France with his long-estranged mother and her new, rich husband, after a bitter parting with his father, not knowing that he's dying. It was a bittersweet book, thought provoking, bringing to light both the dichotomy of life, the good and the bad, the happy and the sad… and the ultimately unresolved question of why things are the way they are. A particular quote that I remember is "그대**가** 헛되이 보낸 오늘은, **어제** 죽어간 이가 **그토록** 살고 싶어하던 내일". In English, I translate it as "This day you lived so carelessly is the tomorrow a dying person of

10

yesterday yearned to live." It's a poignant phrase, isn't it? Live life to the fullest, everyone out there. Do something with it.

What have I lived? I've lived an ordinary life, I guess, with it's ups and downs... But a particular fortnight was an experience I'll never forget. Year 10 was the year I was one of ten Korean students chosen from Australia to participate in a cultural scholarship to Korea for two weeks, and met people from all over the world who were just like me. Ordinary Korean teens living their lives away from Korea, in places like Canada, France, Germany, Spain, Brazil, Singapore, Madagascar... Here, we were all the same in having had similar experiences, having struggled to hang on to our Korean heritage in our respective foreign countries. During this trip, back in Korea, we explored our homeland, or cultural and ethnic roots.

Year 10 was the year of my 'cultural emancipation', for the lack of any other expression. It was the year I came to accept, if not completely understand, the "why" behind the weekly ritual of Korean School on Saturdays, of always speaking in Korean at home, of having to read Korean books, to learn Korean-Chinese characters.

Year 10 was the year I came to accept the need to hold on to my Korean cultural identity. Why? You might as well ask me why the world's the way it is.
But see – I *know*.
I know that no matter how hard, tiresome and futile it seems to learn a language you don't use nearly as often as the language used where you live, it's necessary.
I know that it's necessary, because even if we only ever use that language at home, or with other Koreans, it's a way of celebrating who we are, and what we're a part of.
I know that you can't forsake your ethnicity, even if you want to.
I know that no matter where we live, what we do, *we are Korean.*

Do you want the ending to the story about the little girl?

Keep the curtains open, tie them back.
The show will go on.

11

"A Girl Down Under"

This is me, the girl laughing with her Australian friends, all of them – Korean, Chinese, Indian, Anglo-Saxon.
I'm sixteen, I live in Australia, I'm Korean – I'm on the top of the world.

This story has yet to end.

"From Bergen Academy to Korea and Back"

Joon Park (Bergen Academy, New Jersey, USA)

I sit in my room and wonder where all the boxes of Korean herbal medicine are. You see, my grandmother is neurotic about my height. For some reason, she believes that this Korean herbal medicine will make me into a Yao Ming, but I hate the stuff. Why? You have to understand how it is to know why nobody in his right mind would love this medicine. To start, this Korean herbal medicine is comprised of different components that I cannot identify. I know there is ginseng in there somewhere because all Korean herbal medicines contain some

13

ginseng. Each packet of daily dosage comes with brown and black bits and pieces of something, thrown together and wrapped in a paper pouch. Each time my mom opens the pouch and heats it, as it is the custom, I wonder if there is a piece of dog ear and bear toenail and even maybe some disgusting part of a plant anatomy that are part of the concoction. When the medicine starts boiling, it seems like 5 dead people resurrected with their still-rotting bodies. It gets worse when I taste the medicine. It tastes worse than it smells. Even when I block my nose, I can still smell and tasted it. My grandmother is convinced that this will make me grow.

This summer, I went to Korea. My grandmother fed me this Korean medicine every day. I don't know if I even grew a millimeter as I drank this every day, but I became convinced of one thing – it was not because my grandmother hated me that she sent this Korean herbal medicine. She loves me, and in her own way, the herbal medicine is the ice cream that western grandmothers buy their grandsons. I guess culture explains the difference in love. Koreans believe true love is helping someone improve, whereas, from my understanding, the western notion of love is to make the other person feel good.

However, westernization must have entered, because my grandmother shows me love in the western style. She lets me see all the TV I want to see. Just like too much ice cream is not good, too much TV isn't good, either. But like the Western grandmother who likes to spoil her grandson, my Korean grandmother spoiled me silly this summer, by letting me do just about anything, except for not drinking the Korean herbal medicine. For, my grandmother could not completely give up her Korean ways.

I guess I needed my grandmother's love this summer, both the spoiling kind of the Western tradition, and the unalterable Korean kind of force feeding me the Korean medicine. Both helped me realize that my grandmother truly loves me – and wants me to be happy in life.

I realized while experiencing the love of my grandmother in Korea why I needed that kind of spoiling love. You see, for the whole year, starting from September 2007 to June 2008, I worked very hard to get into Bergen Academy, an elite high school in Bergen County, New Jersey, and to prepare for high school.

The idea of applying to Bergen Academies (there are several different types of schools, focusing on science or the arts, etc., which form the elite institution) reached me when multiple people tried to persuade me into applying. I enjoyed the sciences, so it pleased me greatly to find that the school had the resources and education to provide a fun, top-notch level of education in the sciences.

I immediately set out on trying to become accepted to the science-oriented Bergen Academy. I studied extremely hard, every day. I sent my application form in the fall.

My mother played a huge role in assisting me. I thought that my mom's greatest deed for me was morally supporting me. There was a time, during the process of studying, when I thought of giving up everything and going to my local high school. The pressure was too much, and I began to lose more and more sleep. I was a lost boat in a sea of despair. However, I saw a light – a ray of hope shining onto me, from my mom's support. She was the lighthouse that led me out of the sea and back onto shore. I regained my footing and then was able to work hard again.

The time between the sending of the application and taking the exam, I used to study and learn even more about the school. It became time to take the entrance exam – and I found that all my studying paid off. The math test was relatively simple – 40 questions with 3 optional open-ended at the end. After the math test, I had to read a story about a boy's hatred for and relationship with his "guacamole-colored" jacket. I then wrote an essay describing the relationship the boy had with his jacket. I breezed through this section since I read many books before the exam. Finally, there was the interview. I could see nervousness around everyone – locked jaws, fidgety hands, constantly moving bodies. The interview as not exactly an interview – I had to talk about my partner's traits to the teachers, who were jotting down notes. After the exam, my loss of patience and the increasing amount of suspense rose after each passing day.

Finally, the next month, I found the envelope containing the results. I was full of joy from seeing the mail. However, the joy quickly subsided when I realized that there was still a chance for me to get rejected. I looked at the envelope. It was thin – a possible rejection note. My hands trembled like an earthquake, and I was sweating up a tsunami. I held up the mail to the sun in possible hope that I might be able to read it. Anxiety and curiosity took control of my body and I tore open the envelope. I was reading the letter, and my heart was racing. The

following words popped out at me while I quickly scanned the letter –
"Congratulations, accepted, see you this year."

I breathed a sigh of great relief. I became so happy I thought I
would be able to jump up high and reach the sky. By the time it was
summer vacation, I was in a very happy mood and was ready to leave for
my vacation to Korea. It was at that moment, with my acceptance behind
me that I felt the overwhelming pressure that had mounted over the year
as I prepared for the process of getting in to Bergen Academy. My
grandmother's spoiling love was, therefore, just what I needed to
"recharge" and be ready for my year at the Bergen Academy.

I stayed with my grandmother for three weeks while in Korea, I
can remember one special trip to the idyllic surroundings of Taegu,
South Korea, where all my Korean relatives live. It began with an early
morning wake-up call from my wonderful grandmother who wanted to
show her world to me. My eyelids felt extremely heavy. But, when I
gazed up with my eyes half open and saw my grandmother's excitement
and desire to have a fun trip with me, I could not but feel loving warmth
heating up my heart and filling it with growing excitement.

I prepared for the journey my grandmother had in wait for me. I
ran down the flights of stairs, to the base floor, into the cozy, green car.
My mother, grandmother, brother, and my aunt, the driver, were waiting
for me. The car began to move and then I was off to one of my most
special trips in Korea. The long journey seemed like a second because I
was asleep.

When I woke up refreshed, I awoke to a whole new world. The
magnificent mountainsides were carpeted with hundreds of shades of
green trees. Beyond the mountains was a golden, glowing sun that I
thought resembled my mood at the time. We were treated to the sweet,
dulcet scent of nectar. I heard many birds chirping (one of which I
identified as a cuckoo bird), and busy bees buzzing, trying to gather as
many pollen and nectar as possible. Near where the car was parked, there
was a playful doe for the festive enjoyment of mother nature. The
surrounding mountains blew us a welcoming kiss. To complete the
magical atmosphere were flora and fauna that rainbowed around us. I felt
loved in the midst of all the people who love me most in the world. My
mother, who is my guiding angel in life, was standing by me, and I could
feel the warmth of her loving gaze. My grandmother was on the other
side of me, matching my mother's love. My older brother, who is like my

bodyguard, making me completely protected, was standing in front of me, as if to ward off any evil that may creep into this beautiful scenery. My father's sister was there as a wonderful tour guide. I felt that my father, who was back in the USA working hard, was with us in spirit because of the facial resemblance that I saw in his sister.

I found that the idyllic voyage was only the beginning of my exciting time in Taegu (actually, pronounced "Daegu" in Korean). Daegu is famous as a tourist site because of its beautiful beaches. I was excited for my first day at Daegu beach, Korea. When I arrived, it was very different from beaches in America. The first thing I noticed were vendors – there were stands lined up around the beach. Some of the stands even had people to advertise on the beach. Some of the things the stands sold were chicken, drinks (cider, water, or coke). The most popular stand was the tube, parasol and mat renting. Altogether (they didn't rent separately) the tube-parasol-mat collection was around 10,000 Won (approx. $10). My brother rented the pack, and I entered the sand. I found the sand grains of Daegu beach very smooth. It felt a bit like walking on a blanket. The sand was extremely hot, so I had to keep running so as not to burn my feet. The beach itself had people everywhere. Nearly everyone had the rent package, and there were parasols open everywhere. There were about 3 people per 10 feet. The ocean was extremely clean – clean enough to see the bottom lined with seaweed. There were many people floating on tubes – those closest to the shore got battered with waves. The waves were about 6 inches tall, but occasionally, waves over 1 ft came. I stepped into the water. The water was as cold as ice. As I got further away, I found the floor was significantly cooler than near the surface. On my tube, the scene went up and down from the waves.

Besides the wonderful beaches of Daegu, another attraction that held us in enthrall was their grandiose amusement part, called Woobang Tower Land (Woobang is a district of Daegu). Woobang Tower Land was a ghost town when I first entered. I figured so, since I came at the time when everyone had finals for their school (summer vacation did not start yet for Korean students, who only get about half the time off for summer, compared to American students). While I was riding the cable car to the central tower, I looked down at all the rides and stands. They were like flowers, scattered, unique, and colorful around an area. At the top of the tower, everything was small – like dolls and dollhouses. The

17

rides did not seem so fun with nobody riding, so I came back again after the summer break started for Korean students.

When I returned, I still had a phobia of rollercoasters, but somehow my brother was more determined this time to get me to experience the "joys of rollercoaster rides." I was spectating the queue for the rollercoaster named, "Camelback". I watched the passengers of the ride scream, and I shuddered as I watched the car drop into a steep abyss. Suddenly, I heard my brother's voice, "You should try the rollercoaster. If you don't, I *will* call you a chicken for the rest of your life." I hesitated, but then I felt a shove from my brother. All of a sudden, I became one of the passengers for the rollercoaster. I screamed at my brother as the car started going up the hill. It took a while for it to reach the top, where I could see the whole park. The car began to turn into the very same hill as the one I saw earlier. I closed my eyes tightly and screamed as I felt the heavy drop. It was so fast, I nearly lost my hat. The rollercoaster went up and down (hence the name, "Camelback"). It went into a twist and then the car rolled into a wide turn. By the time I opened my eyes (they were closed the whole ride), the ride was already over. I was recovering from the adrenaline rush, until my brother told me that I had to ride the roller coaster again. Before I had the time to protest, I was pushed back into the car, this time with my brother sitting next to me (watching to see if I had my eyes closed or not). I was back up on the familiar hill. I was about to close my eyes again, but my brother yelled at me and ordered me to keep them open the whole ride. I suppose I had to obey, as my brother was older than me (by 6 years). Since I was used to all the twists and turns of the ride, the ride was not so scary with my eyes open. Next to me, I heard my brother chuckle about how boring the ride was. The car came to a halt at the station, and my brother and I got off. That is the most memorable experience from Woobang Tower Land.

My Korean trip, which was a type of an exciting roller coaster ride, came to an abrupt end after three weeks, when we had to go back to America. A large group of my family seeing us off at the West Incheon International Airport made the departure less painful. The business class seats were comfortable, and I felt cradled in business seats fit for royalty. My royal throne made the pain less poignant. The stewardesses in the aircraft were all wearing a red outfit that was trimmed with white. There was a particular one who served me throughout the ride. She was pretty and young, in her mid-20's. She was about 5'6". She had very dark brown hair. She always had a smile, which reminded me of the cheshire cat from the Disney movie, "Alice in Wonderland." She brought me meals.

The lunch was comprised of rice, seasoned beef (otherwise known as "bulgogi" in Korean), and a side dish of vegetables (including kimchi, which is spiced nappa cabbage). Included in the lunch were spices, but I chose not to use them because I am unable to eat spicy food, having been in America too long. Since I skipped breakfast, I was very hungry, and I enjoyed eating the food. For a meal served on a plane, the dish was quite exquisite. When I was done with the meal, I killed time by watching documentaries. Some were on mythology, and some were on the theory of evolution. I looked over at other business passengers and they were busily typing on their laptops. I looked over at my brother, who was snoring so loudly that nearby passengers were forced to use their earplugs. The last sound I heard before falling into a deep sleep was the low hum of the aircraft engine (combined with my brother's snores). When I woke up, the plane arrived on U.S. Soil. I could see the JFK airport outside.

After I arrived in the U.S., I thought about what I liked about Korea. First, I realized that Korea has very cheap prices on ice cream. I was shocked to have found out that 20 ice cream bars cost just 5 USD. Secondly, it was nice to see my family and all the positive changes that have occurred to my relatives. For example, it was nice to see how my cousin, a baby in my previous visit, knew how to talk. Another reason I liked my trip to Korea was that I got to go to a Korean beach for the first time. It was good to see Korea and feel that I am connected to this land, although I don't understand the language perfectly, and I cannot eat all the spicy food.

All my relatives are in my Korea, so technically, Korea is more of a home for me than America, although I feel more comfortable in America. Although I annoyed my relatives every time we were at a restaurant because I requested from the waiters to take out all the hot spices, seeming almost non-Korean to the waiters, who might have thought that I was used to bland Japanese food like a Japanese person, had I not been with my relatives, I still felt accepted in the midst of all the teasing and laughing. I have to confess that I experienced my Korean identity most poignantly during this summer trip to Korea, and I thank my parents for the opportunity to enjoy Korea and understand my Korean identity better.

"My Korean-Indian Experience and Why I Want to Help People"

Jung-Im Jeong (Canadian International School, INDIA)

"Jung-Im will now come out and say her last goodbye to everyone here," announced my 1st grade teacher in Korea.

I still remember very vividly how my first day was so close to my last day in my school in Korea. I remember how I walked towards the front of the class after my teacher called me forward to say my last goodbye. While I talked about how I had enjoyed the class for past two weeks, few of my classmates started to cry. This is all I remember of my life in Korea right before leaving for India.

Although it was only 8 years of living in Korea, I still remember my life routines in Korea. Every weekend for me was family time, where my grandparents and my cousins all got together and had a lot of fun altogether. Our family as a whole big group held picnics, went for vacations to beaches, and had lot of fun sharing stories, etc. Not only that, at least once a week my parents took me for a children's play where I was able to participate in a proper visual experience to understand the children's books I used to read. The play's title changed every week, and it was normally from fairy tales or well-known folk tales.

Every Sunday was a church day where our family all went together to the church and interacted with a lot of other families. Church was also one of the places where I made a lot of family friends. Since Korea is the most Protestant Christian nation in Asia, with already two Presbyterian elders being Presidents (one of whom is the current South Korean president), since the beginning of the modern country of Korea in 1945, many Koreans are found in Presbyterian churches in South Korea on Sundays. So, many businessmen, politicians, intellectuals, and academics socialize in churches on Sundays.

During my weekdays, I had piano classes, art classes and ballet classes after my kindergarten. I was thankful to belong to a privileged family, which can offer me all the lessons that I wanted in all kinds of cultural and intellectual activities. Basically my life was like a life of a princess from an elite family. I experienced no hardship in life and my family did not have any financial problems. So, I never knew what it was like to be financially unstable.

India was the place where I encountered difficulty because most of the country is so poor. It was not difficulty belonging to my family or our family's social relations (we associated mostly with elite people in India), but the poverty of the landscape was a significant change from the polite bustle of the wealthy metropolis of Seoul, South Korea.

21

"My Korean-Indian Experience and Why I Want to Help People"

I can honestly say that India is where I developed as a person. And India is where most of my life that I can remember took place. Although I had no choice in moving to India, I am glad that my family moved to India. I have come to understand poverty and the need to alleviate poverty around the world. I would have never come to this realization had I remained in my privileged cocoon in South Korea. I know that I want to help people throughout my life because of what I have seen and experienced in India.

Our family had to move to India because of my father's executive job with Samsung. Samsung was expanding as a global company, and Samsung needed a trusted manager to lead the Samsung IT division, newly opened in Bangalore, India. My father, Hae Ryong Jeong, was the one chosen to lead the new Samsung team in the important IT sector.

I guess one part of me was full of excitement when I came to know that I was moving to India. I was very eager to know how the place I would live would look like and how my life in new country would be like. As a little girl, I was fascinated that I was going on an airplane to a completely new place to live. I guess you can say that I had a Little Princess attitude about India. I did not know about the abject poverty of the country.

Understandably, the excitement did not last long. When I arrived in India, I was inundated with images of poverty, which I did not know how to compute as a young privileged girl of 8. Due to the great change in my lifestyle and changes in my surrounding, such as horrible condition of water, food, etc. everywhere in public places, I started to get really sick very often. My first period in the morning at school started in the nurse's office because I would get sick due to the 40 minutes car ride in the morning from home to school; I felt sick at all the poor people in dirty clothes walking everywhere in the streets, poor girls doing headstand in the middle of running traffic for a few coins, cars running pell-mell, not obeying road laws, and fumes from unregulated smog and pollution.

In Korea, it was just a 10 minute walk to school and everything was clean and people wore clean, nice clothes, but in India nothing was possible without transportation, especially because the roads are bad and dirty with poor people everywhere.

And it did not help that I did not speak English, which is the official language of India (along with Hindi). I felt like a deaf-mute who was taking a safari ride through earthly hell. When I arrived in India, I had a very small knowledge of English. Only things I knew how to say were: 'Hello,' 'How are you,' 'Thank you,' 'My name is …' and several other basic sentences. Because of my poor English ability, all the Korean friends whom I had made started avoiding me because they would get in trouble often due to my asking them during class what many things said by the teacher meant in Korean. As time passed, my Korean friends became further annoyed and told me bluntly that they would not talk to me unless I spoke in English. This was the time when I made up my mind firmly and decided to learn English.

At first it was hard to construct sentences by trying to translate each word from Korean to English and trying to find the right and easy words to translate into. But if it were not for this method, my English would not have improved that fast. I was soon able to communicate with others in English and did not become sick as often. This helped me to make lot of friends, and I was able to become rank 1 in class after a year.

If I think back about my Korean friends during my first year, I thank them now because it was they who made me practice English and gave me the eagerness and enthusiasm to learn English faster. I realize now that the right kind of make can make a world of difference. Effective help can make a deaf-mute person into a number 1. And my desire to help others formed after my first year in India.

My desire to help people became more poignant when I beheld poverty in India on a daily basis. It was a shock for me to see the great amount of population in need of help. Living in Korea, I had not much opportunity to experience lot of beggars in streets and little girls carrying a baby and asking for money. There were a lot of people in need of help, but I did not know what to do but to be surprised and shocked. It was then, I resolved that I was going to find a way to help poor people in India or wherever I end up living the rest of my life.

I took my first step to helping people by participating in a short-term missions trip by my church in India, Bangalore Korean Church, which is the biggest Korean-speaking Presbyterian church in Bangalore, India. It was my third year in India when my church went on a missionary camp to a city called Andhra Pradesh in India. By that time, I was almost completely adjusted to India with many different experiences

23

and felt that I knew the country much better. During the short missions trip, we visited many different churches in villages where big groups of Indians would all sit on the ground and worship Jesus Christ. They did not have houses that we have, they did not have the cars that we have, they did not have the accessories we have, nor did they have electronics, even such basic things as light generated by electricy, like we have. Looking at these people, worshipping Jesus Christ with a sincere heart and great enthusiasm, moved me greatly and made me feel like helping them in any kind of way.

My father, who is an Elder of Bangalore Korean Church, was also really touched as well by how Christianity gave the poor Indians joy and hope in life to give them meaning in life. Thus, my dad decided to personally finance building more than 100 Presbyterian churches in India. There are thousands and thousands of Indian Christians without a church building that they could call their own. My dad has already started the process and has built almost ten churches in India already. I guess I am my father's daughter. I have his spirit to help others and bring happiness to others.

One particular thing during the missions trip especially moved me. It happened at one particular Indian church that we went to. It was one of the smallest churches that I have seen in my life; it was a one-room church. But I consider it a decisive turning point in my life.

After half of the people entered the church, rest of the people had to stay outside because there was not enough space for everyone. The church service was almost over, and it was offering time. There was an old lady who was standing nearby me. Her health seemed to be not in a good shape. Her back was not straight, she was too skinny, and she had trouble walking normally. I clearly remember her missing fingers on her left hand. With her hands, she took out a two rupee coin from a small tiny purse that could fit two to three more coins. It was all she had, but she still donated it to Jesus Christ. She was praising God and happy to donate to the ministry of the Word and Sacrament. It was obvious that she valued the church of Jesus Christ more than anything in the world. She might have to miss some meals because of that donation to Christ Jesus. She may have to go hungry for a few days. But she was filled with joy. It was a testimony to her faith in Christ and love or Christ's church.

I did not know what to do with my eyes, which were full of tears. She had sacrificed her whole money, and this Christian faith and devotion really touched me. I then felt a really strong desire to help. And I really wanted to help all others out there and do something for them. Our family approached the old woman and offered her money so she could have a more comfortable life, but she refused to take the money. For her, she was joyful at having given her all to her Savior and LORD Jesus Christ. It was a sign of her love for the One who had saved her from eternal damnation and given her eternal life. For her, what was really important was her relationship with Jesus Christ and working hard to build His Church in her neighborhood. For her, the church of Jesus Christ was more important than her own well-being. For her, Jesus Christ was the source of her joy and she would gladly give her all to honor Christ Jesus. Her donation to the church was born out of love, faith, and devotion. She did not want any of her devotion to Christ to be taken away, even though it meant eating better and having a better life.

Refusing money in India was something new. In a sense, I was really surprised by it. In India, wherever we went, there were beggars and a lot of people in need of help, asking for money. I would never forget that old lady in my life, who is a testimony to the Christian faith and the power of the joy in Jesus Christ. Christianity brings hope and joy to people. Because my father realized this, he had committed himself to building 100 Christian churches in India. It is the hope that the Christian church offers to poor Indians that is more important to them than life itself and all the wealth in the world. I could see that many in the crowded church in one of the poorest neighborhoods in India shared her joy in being saved through the substitutionary death of Jesus Christ on the cross in Jerusalem. I feel that I became a better Christian as the result of her faith and devotion to Jesus Christ.

I realized the power of hope in the midst of poverty. I realized the power of the Christian faith to change people's lives for better. There are more important things in life than food, shelter, and clothing. Sometimes, humanitarians miss the point. People are not happy because they have food, clothing, and shelter; people are happy because they have salvation in Jesus Christ and a concrete hope for the future. I would like to help others to come to know Jesus Christ as their personal Savior. And like Jesus Christ, I would like to help the poor and the oppressed. I want to find ways to help those who are less privileged and meet the needs of those who lack.

I feel most fortunate to be attending Canadian International School, which is one of the most elite schools in India. I know that the elite education that I receive at Canadian International School and the education I will receive in the future in university will help me to be a better leader to help the poor, the downtrodden, and the non-privileged. Like St. Francis of Assisi who came from a very privileged background who ended up helping the poor and giving them hope, I would like to be highly educated to help the poor and the weak. Thus, my education holds special meaning and purpose for me.

I have lived in India for the past 11 years, and my feeling towards the people in need of help is still the same. For the past 11 years, I have been seeing so many different kinds of beggars. Every stop I make at the signals, I come across at least one or two beggars. Despite the fact that I see them every day, I still do get tears in my eyes. The fact that I cannot really do much for them right now just hurts me. Giving money to beggars in India is not recognized as a good thing because it is a part of a type of organized crime where they have to pay their "boss" all their money gathered through begging. Churches are the best way to help the poor in India, and I tithe and give donation to Bangalore Korean Church to help in my church's effort to help the poor of Bangalore, India.

There are many heart-breaking things in the streets of India. There are even little kids who show little tricks to ask for money, and there are little girls who sometimes even rent babies and use them to gain sympathy. There are old men and women who don't have one arm or are limping with their skinny legs. Looking at these people for the past 11 years, I still can't get used to it, and I hope that I will never get used to it. I want to help the poor, the weak, and the disenfranchised throughout my life, and I want to have the heart of my LORD and Savior Jesus Christ.

My experiences involving my desire and determination for helping others, I would say, were a part of the fundamental roots that started shaping me as a person.

In terms of education, two schools provide me with the education to get to where I want to go. The Korean School run by the Korean Community Center of Bangalore, India, which my father helped to found (my dad was the President of the Bangalore Korean Community

Center) and Canadian International School, which provides elite private school education in Bangalore, India.

Bangalore Korean Community Center, under my dad's direction and inspiration, pro-actively sponsors The Korean School for the education of Korean youth in Korean language, culture, and history. Every Saturday I had Korean school with almost 100 other Korean students in a rented Indian school building. There were classes from kindergarten to middle school. There, I interacted with many different Koreans with different Indian experiences and perspectives. Some students viewed India as just a poor country or dirty country and others viewed it as a country where it was a lot more comfortable than Korea (all Koreans live an elite existence in India by India's standards with chauffer-driven cars and top-end housing, which their parents' Korean companies pay for besides their salary and other compensation for working in India). It was the Korean school that helped me to understand how schools in Korea operated since there was a constant flow of Koreans into India at all age group levels and school grade levels. And the Korean school helped me to not forget my own language. It is very easy to forget a language when you leave the country where the language is spoken in the first grade. Without Korean school, my Korean skills would have degenerated from 1st grade level to almost non-existence. I have heard that many Koreans who go to the USA in 1st grade completely forget Korean by the time they are seniors in high school.

The most fun part of the Korean school was the sports day. Apparently, sports day is an integral part of the Korean school system. Although the sports day in Korea is really different from the sports day of my Korean school in Bangalore, India, I still have a clear idea of how sports day is ran in Korea all because of my experiences in my Korean school in Bangalore, India, which always tries to recreate the sports day in the fashion of the sports day of schools in Korea. Also, the Korean school in Bangalore, India, provides a detailed explanation of what sports day is like in Korea, every year. The experiences in the Korean school helped me a lot to develop sportsmanship since I was young. I also learned a lot of creative things during the extracurricular time, like what students in Korea enjoy doing and what is important to them. At the Korean School in Bangalore, India, there were violin class, sign language class, needle work class, tae kwon do class, sa mul nori class (which is basically Korean traditional music group), and many more programs. I

27

was able to experience most of them during my nine years of Korean school in Bangalore, India.

Besides the Bangalore Korean Community Center Korean School, I was educated by Canadian International School in Bangalore, India, which is one of the most elite private international schools in India.

Now picture an international school in southern India run by Canadians. The first thing that comes to one's mind may be classrooms full of students and teachers of different ethnic backgrounds or a sports field where cricket and soccer are played side by side. Variety would definitely be one of the more special features of the school. Of course, there are other attractions such as teachers with a global perspective, friends with distinct cultures to share, and sunny weather throughout the year. The school sounds like a pretty interesting place to be, with a lot to offer to the students. As one may have guessed it already, I am describing my own school. Before you jump to conclusions, I am not here trying to tell you how great my school is, though it is definitely a pretty good place to be as a student. For the most part, Canadian International School is great. But what I want to say is more specific and has to do with the less attractive side of the school, precisely because it is an international school: Constant changes that happen there.

Unlike most of my friends, I have been going to the same Canadian International School (CIS) in Bangalore, India, for the past eleven years. So, you can say that I am a Canadian International School "product." So far, I know of only one person in the whole school who has been at the school as long as I have. The students at CIS usually stay only for two to three years and four years if long, and they would leave afterwards to another country because of their father's job. My friends always left me sooner or later, and each time I was forced to make new friends all over again. At first I had complained quite a bit, but without noticing, I gained greater ability to adapt to changes and to understand many different cultures and at the same time respect them, too. I had developed in a way a talent to adapt and get to know new people more easily and faster. A lot of new people needed a lot of help and I always enjoyed helping them as an experienced person in the school and in the country. In a sense, you can say that I had my first real taste of the joys of helping others at Canadian International School as a veteran of the school.

I realized that social skills I have acquired at Canadian International School was of tremendous benefit in other places as well. For instance, when I participated in summer schools in Stanford University in 2007 and 2008, I was quick at adapting to my environment. I had gone to summer programs, called Junior Statesman of America for two summers, but I had no problem making new friends and excelling in their program. Although the summer course was to experience a university life with intensive academic work, I managed to adapt and was surprised at myself as well for becoming so popular with American students and American professors. Before going to my first summer school at Stanford, I thought it would be hard as when I first arrived in India from Korea, but I realized that I had blossomed into a leader who can quickly gain the respect of my peers and the adoration of my teachers, even in a culture completely different from Korea and India, or Canada, for that matter. I had learned a lot from all the different cultures and understand how careful I need to be at first to respect other cultures and backgrounds. Although there are many different cultures and backgrounds at Canadian International School, I realized how all of us have something in common. We all laugh and know how to have fun all together. No different language was needed when all of us were laughing and were willing to help each other out. I know that wherever I am, I can not only survive, but also be a leader because I have proven that at two summer schools at Stanford with two different groups of students. And I continue to fill leadership role at Canadian International School, by helping newly arriving Korean students and also in official capacity as a member of the Student Council. I am grateful to God for bringing me to India because now I respect other cultures more and have developed into an international leader at my young age.

And ironically, I believe that I am more aware of the Korean culture than the Koreans who actually live in Korea. I can compare Korean culture with Indian culture, Canadian culture, and now American culture. I can see the subtle differences, and I can explain the difference. I have developed a critical ability to understand my culture that is missing from people who do not have an experiential opportunity to compare their own culture with those of others in a completely submerged setting. Because of my experiences, I can see everyone from outside the box and see the difference between how Koreans react to certain things and how non-Koreans react to certain things.

29

"MY KOREAN-INDIAN EXPERIENCE AND WHY I WANT TO HELP PEOPLE"

Not only that, being outside of Korea means that I can be a cultural ambassador for Korea. I took part in several Korean traditional ceremonies and performances as a cultural ambassador to showcase Korean culture to non-Koreans. Koreans in Korea do not have this opportunity. When my father was the Bangalore Korean Community Center president in India, he started an event, to which all Indians were invited. We prepared hard and were able to show our culture and traditions by tae kwon do (Korean martial arts) demonstrations, traditional dances, traditional dress fashion shows, Sa Mul Nori drumming shows, etc. I was grateful enough to participate in sharing the beauty of Korean culture with non-Koreans. I was able take part in tae kwon do, the fashion show, and Sa Mul Nori. With these abilities, I was also able to show our Korean traditions to my Indian and Canadian international school friends at the multicultural days.

In my international school, I like taking part in many different activities because I really do enjoy helping people and contributing something to the society so that people would benefit and I too would feel very happy about myself. Some examples are my experience in the Student Council as a secretary, my experience in Model United Nations conferences, experience in the school choir, helping the drama crew by having the privilege to become the stage manager for a Shakespeare play, helping elementary teachers with their extracurricular activities such as cooking and gymnastic, getting peer helper certificate after going through several workshops, etc.

My friends and I enjoyed feeling good about ourselves by helping people, so we visited orphanages and a local school to teach French. The most memorable moment in the orphanage visit was a baby who was just two years old. The baby could barely open her eyes and was too small for me to carry. The orphanage told us how the baby was just found in the streets and was immediately brought to the orphanage. We were told that this happens a lot in India. All the babies in the orphanage needed a lot of care and love, and I really wanted to do give something more to them, always.

I also had a memorable experience at a local school. The principal of Canadian International School wanted me and my friend to teach something new to the students at the extracurricular time, and we decided that French would be something really new for them and that they would enjoy learning it.

30

We started with very basics in French with a lot of worries because France could even be a country that the local Indian students have never heard before. Going beyond our expectations, the students there were just fascinating. They were very well aware of what France was and were very motivated to learn French that it brought all my energy out to teach them. The local Indian students thanked us earnestly, and it really did mean a lot for me. This experience helped me to be happy. As I went through all these experiences, I came to reaffirm my goal and desire to help people throughout my life. I want to be something positive in their lives as they mean a lot in my life. I value and treasure all those who are in need of help, whatever that may be.

I spend much time at Bangalore Korean Church, where I am the Youth Group president right now, because my church was the starting point for me to realize that I wanted to help people. I also wanted to contribute something to my church in response. As the president of the BKC Youth Group, I help new Korean students who arrive to feel a part of the community and encourage harmony between Koreans with different backgrounds and interests. I like helping people when they are new to India because I know how it feels like to be at a completely new place, some even without family, due to my experience of adjusting to India and to America. I know they would not feel so comfortable approaching someone new and asking for help, so I always approach the new people and try to get to know them better and see if they need any help or not.

I believe that to be a resourceful person and a reliable person, I need to gain people's trust first for them to approach me more easily and let me help them as much as I could. In order to be that particular kind of person, I try to keep my academic standards higher than average. I've always managed to stay in the upper half of the honor roll list in my school, and in my junior year, I was even able to make it to the principal's list. With this academic confirmation, even teachers now recommend to other students to seek help from me at Canadian International School. I proudly take the chances gratefully and try my best to help them at my maximum level.

Hence, I would like to say that I do love helping people, and it is really worth it because not only do I benefit from feeling happy and proud, but others too benefit. I really like how people in need of help in some way take part in my life, and in return I try to be part of their lives

"My Korean-Indian Experience and Why I Want to Help People"

by helping them at the best level that I could. Helping others, I would say, is how I find myself worth living.

"My Life as a Korean in Korea"

Timothy Chon (Charles DeWolf Middle School, New Jersey, USA)

"Hurry up! We have to leave to go to school soon," yelled my mother. I got out of bed and started to get dressed.

"This is crazy," I thought to myself. "How am I supposed to have a nice vacation when I have to go to school?" Today is the first day that I have to go to school in Seoul, Korea. I have to go to school because my Korean is not *good enough* for my parents. This was in the year 2007 on July 15th.

While I was getting ready, my brother just stayed in bed and just laid there like a lazy person. At times like this, my mom would tell me to make him get out of bed. At these terms, I would go up to him, take the

33

covers off, and hit him right on the chest. When I do that, he either punches me back, or stays in bed. Usually, I just wait until my mom yells at him to get out or he gets up on his own.

After we dress up and get ready, we go downstairs to the lobby of the Marriot Hotel and eat at the breakfast buffet. Usually, we go down at around eight o'clock. Most of the time, I just go get cereal, bacon, an omelet with ham, Cheddar cheese, and egg. At this time, there are usually about twenty people. There is a chef who makes the omelet and about five trays of different food such as pancakes, French toast, bacon, and scrambled egg.

At around eight-thirty, we go outside to catch a taxi. When we do catch a taxi, I sit in the middle with my mom on the left and my brother on the right. It takes about 20 minutes to get to the school, which is called Ma-Poe Elementary School. Since it takes some time to get there, I usually sleep. Sometimes I would listen to my Ipod on the way there.

School starts at 9:00 A.M. Before I came in the building, I had to wear special kind of shoes. Regular shoes were prohibited. I think they had this rule because they did not want to get the school full of dirt and other things from the shoes that we regularly wear. I go to class and am bored most of the time. Luckily, I have a teacher who speaks English. I forget what her name was, but she looked like she is in her 30's, is about five feet three, and looked like she weighed about 110 pounds. I was impressed that she could speak fluent English. The person who sits next to me is a kid who speaks very little English, but is somewhat helpful. I did not get to find out his name. He was about four feet four, and weighed about 65 pounds.

The school was three stories high and was as long as half a football field. During the actual school day, I usually just sit there and daydream. There is absolutely nothing to do there. Most of the activities we do there in class, I usually sit out for two reasons. One, I don't know how to play, and two, most of the games are boring. The only thing that I actually enjoy there is what happens about two to three times a day. During this time, we play this game where we throw a ball at each other. This game is exactly like dodge ball. If we hit them, they are out of the game. If they catch it, the thrower is out of the game. I was actually able to catch some of the balls that they threw.

For lunch we get a variety of food from the school's cooks. My favorite was when I got to eat spicy tofu soup, which surprisingly tasted pretty good. Other times we would get soup, rice, fish, and other things. We ate in our classroom, which I thought was cool. I really didn't talk with anyone because there was nothing to talk about.

At the end of school, I would meet up with my brother and my friend, Peter, who once was my next door neighbor in Fort Lee, New Jersey, which is in America. He is in the same grade as my brother. My brother and I met him when he moved from Korea in 2002. Then, in 2003, he moved back to Korea because of his dad's job. His dad works as an accountant, which is person who keeps track of other companies' money. He worked for this company for five years. The company he worked at was called "Ernst and Young." Peter also has a little sister in 2nd grade. Her name is Gina. She is about 3"2' and weighs about 55-60 pounds.

After school, we would go down a few blocks and go to a tutor. I took a Korean class which was fairly easy for me. I mainly focused on third and fourth grade math, which was long division, multiplying, adding, subtracting, in order to learn numbers in Korean and Korean math lingo. I did not see the point in going to that place. Before we begin class, the teacher would give me a drink called, "Vita 500." I really enjoy drinking it. It tastes little like Red Bull. I always ask for one more bottle because it is only about 0.7 ounces. Since I am a guest, she usually gives me the second bottle.

At around three o' clock, we would head on to Peter's house to stay there until dinner. We usually just eat and watch TV. We would watch some Korean programs and American movies. The Korean programs are totally weird for me because I couldn't understand most of the things that anyone said or did. For the American programs, I would watch movies like *I, Robot*. Sometimes, we would go play soccer outside for the fun of it. I would play right outside of the building and kick a ball against the wall with Peter and my brother.

Most of the time, we eat with Peter and his family. We either order dinner or go outside to eat. My favorite thing to order is chicken from a place called Kyo Chicken. We ordered fried chicken that tastes like buffalo chicken and some French fries. My favorite place to go to is a noodle restaurant called, "Summer." I usually get thick white noodles, which is called "Udong." The restaurant has about twenty tables and a kitchen. There are about five waiters out at a time, and they all wear an outfit with the color red and blue on it. There are a lot of different dishes, but most of them are entrees that I have never heard of. My brother ordered a thin noodle with black sauce, called "Cha-jong-meung." Peter also got udong and our parents got some other noodles that I have never seen before.

After dinner, we go back to my hotel room at the Marriot Hotel. Most of the time, my brother and I would watch a movie that we brought from the USA. Other times, we go and play poker with Goldfish or go on my dad's laptop and surf around the Internet. Usually we end up playing games. At around nine-thirty, we read a book. I brought the book, *Fire Star*, with me to read. This book is about a person named David Rain, who has clay dragons which are real. He goes through journeys to the Arctic and meets polar bears that are in desperate need.
After about half an hour, we go and brush our teeth, get into our pajamas and go to sleep.

On weekends, we would go to places, like the museum. Sometimes, we would go and meet our relatives who live about an hour away from the hotel. On the first weekend of school, we went to my friend's house. His name was Jack. He is five feet, weighs about 75 pounds and is in 5th grade. He also has an older brother who is in 9th grade. He is five feet seven and weighs about 115 pounds. He usually just stays in his room and listens to his Ipod or watches movies on the computer. Jack and I would go on the computer and watch some videos on a website called "Youtube." Some videos that we watched were called Darth Vader Being a Jerk, Anikin Skywalker being a Jerk, and some other stupid videos. We also would play games like Grand Theft Auto, San Andres. In this game, you are kind of like a hitman and try to get some money. You can also kill people with a gun, hijack cars, and run away from cops. Sometimes we would get bored and go play the Nintendo 64, which is a very old game system that came out in 2001. Jack only had one game which was called, "Pokemon Stadium". In that game, we would play mini games. The one that was hardest for me was to memorize the order of direction. For example, one of them was in the order of left, right, left, up, down, right, down, down , up. Then, we had to press the direction in that order in ten seconds. The game that I liked the most was a game called "Egg Emergency." In this game, we had to put eggs in a pouch that falls from the sky. We have to make it land in a pouch that we hold. We press the left of right button to catch the eggs. The only thing hard about it is that sometimes, electric balls come falling. We want these things to fall and not land in our pouch. Each time an electric ball falls in our pouch, it zaps us and we loose seven eggs. My highest score is one hundred eggs which is a perfect score because there is a total of one hundred eggs that fall.

The next day after we went to Jack's house, we went to a museum that was called "War Memorial Museum." We saw all of the weapons that soldiers used in the Korean War in the 1950's. They used guns, tanks and other destructive weapons, such as bombs. The displayed items that I liked the most were models of army cars and tanks. The army cars were about the size of a mini van. It has a large, open trunk, five seats, and an open top. In the front it had a machine gun, which was pretty cool. The colors were green, dark green, and brown. The tanks were about twice the size of a mini van. We also learned about the story of the Korean War, such as why North Korea attacked the South, how many soldiers died, how long the war was, and other similar questions. North Korea attacked South Korea because they wanted to be one country. I don't remember how many soldiers died, but I remember that over two million people died in South Korea alone. The war lasted from July 25th, 1950 to July 27th, 1953.

On the second weekend of school, we went to our relative's house. The family lived in a town called Mee-La-Lee. They have a small house and a family of five, my uncle, my aunt, and my three cousins. They are related to us because my grandfather and their grandmother are siblings. The first cousin is about 23 years old. Her name is Hong-Mee. She is not married and works at an advertisement company. I am not sure where she went for college. She is tall and looks like she weighs about 110 pounds. The second cousin is 13 years old and is about 5 feet and 2 inches, and he looks like he weighs about 90 pounds. His name is Min-Gyoo. He listens to his father and respects his elders. He is in 8th grade although he looks like he is in 6th. The third cousin is 12 years old and is in 7th grade. She is very kind, and she is gentle with her personal things, like her special vase in her room. I am not so sure why she thinks it is special. Maybe it holds some special value. She attends Young Hoon Middle School. Her name is Min- Gyung. Out of all of them, I like Min-Gyoo the most because we have the most things in common, and he knows what my brother and I like the most as boys. There, we played computer games like, <u>Tekken</u>, on the keyboard. When we got hungry, we took a five minute walk to a nearby store and bought a few bags of chips. Luckily, the chips were very cheap, about one to two dollars for a big bag. For dinner, we ate rice, seaweed, and other Korean food. When we left, our uncle gave us one hundred dollars as a gift. I was so happy that they gave us money for us to use for ourselves on anything we wanted. I decided to save the money for college because until recently, I have been buying a lot of video games and other stuff, instead of saving for important stuff like college.

On the third week, we went to my dad's Uncle's house. He was a famous Korean singer back in the 80's, and he is still well known in Korea. His name is Cho Yong Pil. He is about 5"6' and looks like he weighs about 120 pounds. He has a driver and a cook who looks like they are in their early 30's. The driver wears a black suit all the time. I am not sure what the cook or driver's names are. I don't really know about the cook. As I was walking around the house, I saw about fifty trophies on the wall and on his trophy shelf. A lot of them were written in Korean, so I wasn't able to understand what any of the words meant. He also has about four guitars sitting on stands. One of them was made out of gold. As I was walking around, I overheard my brother asking the driver to show him the cars he had. I decided to go with them. We went downstairs to the garage. He had a Porsche and a Mercedes Benz. The Mercedes Benz was really nice and was a limited edition. It was white, and the seats were very soft and comfortable. I like the Porsche better, though. It felt really good, and it had a really cool engine. I am not sure which parts were what, but it looked really cool with all the pipes and everything was shiny. The driver told us that there are only fifty cars that are exactly the same as that Porsche. The driver took pictures of us in the car. Later, we went back upstairs to eat. We ate shrimp, dumpling soup, and some seaweed with rice. The shrimp was really good because it had good sauce and was cooked very well. The dumpling soup was really good, too. The soup tasted fresh and the dumplings were hot, good tasting, and the meat inside of it was really good.

After the school weeks were over, we went to a place called Eel-San. It was about 300 miles away from Seoul. There, we went hiking up a mountain called Eel-San Mountain. This mountain's path was made by nature. We had to pass streams, rocky paths and climb some steep slopes.

In between the mountains, we saw some statues of Buddha and other statues that looked relatively similar to Buddha. While we were looking at Buddha carvings on the wall, an old man told us about this carving and what it meant. The carving on the stone was about 15 feet high. Buddha had a hat that looks like a crown but without the spikes sticking up. He also had a dot on his forehead. My mom told me that according to something that she read, the bigger the dot on the head, the stronger and more powerful the monk who had the dot was. The carving had Buddha holding up his hand and a few beams coming out of his palm. I wasn't sure how to make out exactly what he was saying, but I know that he said something about Buddha creating everything, like the sun, and how he had power over everything. After the man was finished talking, we continued our journey up the mountain. Later, we saw a man bowing down at a statue. We decided to be very quiet because we didn't want to disturb the man and be rude to him. At one point, we had to climb up a steep rocky slope. Attached to the top was a rope. We took the rope and climbed all the way to the peak. I looked out from the mountain, and we saw everything, such as trees, buildings, and even the next town. After about 15 minutes of rest, we decided to go down the mountain. That took us about an hour and a half. When we arrived at the bottom, we were exhausted and worn out.

On August 22, 2007, we had to go back to the USA. It took us about an hour to get to the airport. When we arrived, we faced security checkpoints. That took us another hour. We waited about 30 minutes before our plane boarded. We rode in business class, which I was grateful for because you get to move your chair around in different positions and relax the whole time. I watched a few movies like "Brain and Bullet," which was about two guys named Brain and Bullet saving a girl from a guy named Winston who wants all of money that the grandfather owns for a business that he wants to make, but it requires a lot of money.

Watching the movies took about four hours out of the 15 hour flight. I slept for about 10 hours because of the time zone difference. But sometimes I woke because they were serving food. The only problem was that the food tasted horrible. They served fish, pasta and scallop. The fish tasted really bland, the sauce for the pasta tasted like it had some oil in it, and the scallop tasted like it was really raw. Therefore, I didn't eat at all. When I felt like I wanted to eat something, I ordered ramen, which is a thin, Japanese noodle.

We were in Korea for a month from mid-July to mid-August of 2007. We went to school for three whole weeks. We only went to school on Saturdays once, though. Although all Korean students go to school on Saturdays, vacation does have its perks. After a while, school got better because I understood a bit more Korean and what the teacher was saying. All in all, I am very happy about my visit to Korea. I feel like I have lived a special life, experiencing the life of a Korean student in Korea, and I thank my parents for this wonderful experience.

"Shakespeare's Support of Traditional Arranged Marriage and the Korean Joong-Mae System"[1]

Paul Sungbae Park (Northern Valley Regional
High School, Old Tappan, New Jersey, USA)

---

[1] I would like to thank Ms. Jennifer Eisgrau of Northern Valley Regional High School, Old Tappan, English Department, who said my research paper is the best that she has ever read in her teaching career and encouraged me.

"SHAKESPEARE'S SUPPORT OF TRADITIONAL ARRANGED MARRIAGE AND THE KOREAN JOONG-MAE SYSTEM"

Romeo and Juliet is a play by William Shakespeare, composed in the Elizabethan Era, to uphold the values of the Elizabethan England, such as traditional arranged marriage, and to oppose romanticization of courtly love. Shakespeare accomplishes this attitude through his characterization of Romeo and Juliet and their love as tragic in the sense that Romeo and Juliet pursued love based on sentimentality and fueled by youthful rebellion against their parents rather than courtly love that is ideal and structured. For Shakespeare, coming from a pro-Elizabethan England morality, the youthful, rebellious love of Romeo and Juliet could only end in tragedy. In his support of traditional arranged marriage, William Shakespeare shows himself to be in agreement with the Joong-Mae System of Korea, which found its rigid formalization in the Yi Dynasty.

Romeo's love for Juliet is fueled by his fickle and sentimental response to Rosaline's rejection, and undergirded by his youthful rebellion to authority. According to Shakespeare, Romeo is a fickle character madly in love with Rosaline. His obsessive pursuit of her resulted in his creation of an "artificial night" to flee from his reality (Shakespeare I.ii.133). Romeo in hiding causes his father to say, "And private in his chamber pens himself, / Shuts up his windows, locks fair daylight out" (Shakespeare I.i.131-2). It is evident that Romeo was emotionally very much involved with Rosaline. Even Benvolio tries to dissuade Romeo from his depression by saying, "Be ruled by me: forget to think of her" (Shakespeare I.i.219).

Although it seems like Romeo had met the love of his life in Rosaline, he is guided by love based on sentimentality as evident in changing his heart right away to Juliet. Romeo meets Juliet at a party scene meant for romance thrown by the Capulets for Paris and Juliet. At the party, he is informed by the Nurse that she is a Capulet daughter. It is because Juliet is a Capulet that he pursues her, and it was his way of rebelling against the authority such as that of the prince. Before the party, there was an altercation scene when Prince warned the two families to be executed if they fought. Romeo also rebelled against his parents, who did not want his son to be near Capulets' vicinity. Romeo also rebelled against the Capulets, who did not want him at the party; the servant carrying the invitation letter says, "If you be not of the house of Montagues, / I pray come and crush a cup of wine" (Shakespeare I.ii.81-2). Guided by his youthful rebellion against authority, Romeo confesses his love toward Juliet after his encounter with Juliet at the party. Besides his rebellious nature, Romeo's love was guided by his desire to escape depression and rejection by Rosaline along with his rebellious nature. Brodwin states, "From the first encounter, however, Romeo conceives of his lady not as an ordinary mortal but as a symbol of divine beauty" (494). His metaphorical usage of the sun proves that he only needed "someone" to love and to love him back. Also, when Juliet asks, "Art thou not a Romeo, and a Montague?" Romeo responds by saying, "Neither fair maid, if either thee dislike" (Shakespeare II.ii.60-1). Romeo wants to persuade Juliet to love him even though she doubts his capability to love her, a Capulet. It was because Juliet was a Capulet that Romeo is motivated to get her love. Even Romeo's priest doubts Romeo's sincerity of love for Juliet; "God pardon sin! / Was thou with Rosaline?" (Shakespeare II.iii.44). In short, Romeo's love was guided by his rebellious and fickle nature, rather than genuine courtly love.

Just as Romeo's love was fueled by sentimentality and rebellion rather than pure romantic love, Juliet's love for Romeo was fueled by her rebellion against authority, including male domination, and her emotional desire to assert her own will. Juliet's love for Romeo began with her rebellious sentiment against her parents' arranged marriage for her. It was often customary during Elizabethan England for marriage to be arranged especially for gaining property or useful political alliances (Stone 42-3). Paris, to whom Juliet's parents wanted to marry Juliet, had both of these traits. Shakespeare portrays Juliet as rebelling against this marriage system. Van Doren explains, "This [arranged marriage] is cynicism though it would be without pornography; at least the young heart of Juliet sees it so" (498). At the party, Juliet was attracted to Romeo's courtship and love advanced because it made her feel like she was in control. To a thirteen year old, who began to open her eyes toward love, Romeo's pursuit put her in the authority position where she could decide to reject or accept him. Brown writes, "During the balcony scene, she can be read as trying to train Romeo. She attempts to make Romeo as obedient as a 'manned' falcon" ("Juliet's Taming of Romeo"). Also, Juliet tells Romeo to deny his name and family (Shakespeare II.ii.39). She is so controlling that she wants Romeo to reject his family and identity, so that all is left of him is their relationship.

Juliet's love is also guided by her rebellion against her mother who set up the arranged marriage for her. Juliet says, "But no more deep will I endart mine eye/ Then your consent gives strength to make it fly" (Shakespeare I.iii.100-1). Although on the surface she seems to be agreeing with her mother, but in reality she is taking matters into her own hands by not protesting. Also, because she is very distant from her mother and because she uses a quite a number of verbal ironies through out the play, she is not revealing her true feelings. An example of this is when Juliet says to her mother, "I will not marry yet. And when I do, I swear/ It shall be Romeo, whom you know I hate" (Shakespeare III.v.120-1).

This is significant in that female teens during Elizabethan England could marry at the age of twelve by law, and most marriages among the English were not arranged by parents (Stewart 23), but instead, Ros describes that it was "generally considered foolish to marry for love…" ("Marriage and Family"). Because this was the reality, Juliet seems like she was taking matters into her own hands by not protesting. Against her father and mother's will of her marrying Paris, she marries Romeo (Shakespeare IV.i.92-100). In marrying Romeo, Juliet rebelled against her parents. MacFarlane writes, "The shift along the continuum from arranged marriage to individual choice has implications for demographic features because it alters the balance within the family" (122). Her marriage was not only a rebellion against her parents but also against the common tradition of the Elizabethan England. Stewart describes the typical understanding of the relationship between love and marriage during his time, "The idea of marrying for love was not common. For a great many people marrying someone was a way to become independent of the parents' home. Most people hoped that once a couple married… love and affection would follow" (23-24).

In the case of Juliet, there was a rebellion against the common mores of the Elizabethan time, in which Shakespeare was writing. Later on, Juliet plans with the Friar to fake her death to escape from Verona and join Romeo. However, Juliet had more options beside betraying her parents and escaping; Cook states, "Under circumstances marriages were annulled, and on a few grounds even a form of divorce was possible" (100). So, Juliet also rebelled by escaping Verona because she had the choice to leave Romeo and marry Paris. Juliet, just like Romeo, pursued love based on sentimentality and youthful rebellion against authority, such as her parents and male domination.

Although Romeo and Juliet's love was driven by sentimentality and rebellion, there are a few aspects of courtly love in the play. For example, the secret nature of their love resembles courtly love. Through the whole secretive planning, Juliet shows herself more interested in rebelling against her parents and what they want from her. Brodwin states, "Her thoughts are driven by a raft of romantic fantasies as she anxiously awaits the return of her confidante, the Nurse, who has been sent to arrange a secret rendezvous with Romeo" (Cook 101). Also, problems that rise throughout the play resemble courtly love. Brodwin writes, "Their love has been born in the heart of obstruction…"(Brodwin 495). As Romeo gets exiled and they suffer missing each other, their bonds strengthen (Brodwin 496). The emotional turmoil shows the struggle many lovers go through in courtly love.

Although the love between Romeo and Juliet resemble some aspects of courtly love, they do not fit courtly love neatly. For example, Romeo and Juliet did not follow the proper procedure of courtly love. Bloom highlights this fact; "Romeo and Juliet's aubade is so disturbingly precise because they are not courtly love sophisticates working through a stylized ritual" (102). Romeo and Juliet's love in some ways resemble more of the "courtship" of today, where teenagers are driven by emotion in pursuit of love without stylized ritual. Cook also elaborates on this fact; "…such intolerance for deviations from normal courting and marriage customs was very strong" (100). Besides not following general procedures for courtly love, Romeo and Juliet, in fact, have secrets from each other due to miscommunication, and this goes against the concept of courtly love where they are supposed to face the world together (Brodwin 493). Lemay discusses the fact that love is working together; "You work at growing, at sharing, at supporting one another through the good times and the bad" ("Star-Crossed-Something or Others"). However, they do not share and support each other. It is because of their digression from the valued principle of sharing secrets together that they end up dying at the end (Shakespeare V.iii.).

In addition, MacFarlane writes, "The second feature of English courtship was its length… the gap between the first meeting and the wedding usually falls between six months and two years (295). However, Romeo and Juliet's gap between their encounter and marriage was only two days, and they therefore broke the normal timeline for proper courtship. Furthermore, Romeo and Juliet do not fit into the concept of courtly love because they are driven by selfish sentimentality and youthful rebellion. Bloom states, *"Romeo and Juliet* is unmatched in Shakespeare and in the world's literature as a vision of an uncompromising mutual love that perishes of its own idealism and intensity" (89). Thus, the outcome of such relationship is death.

Romeo and Juliet's romantic love, which is a protest to the traditional Elizabethan practice of the arranged marriage, is the direct cause of their death. Shakespeare succinctly summarizes the tragedy of Romeo and Juliet's love fueled by sentimentality and youthful rebellion, "whose misadventured piteous overthrows/ Doth with their death bury their parents' strife" (Shakespeare Prologue 8-9). Shakespeare condemns his unfortunate lovers for "thrilling themselves to unhonest desire, neglecting the authority and advice of parents and friends..." (McKittrick). Shakespeare, writing in Elizabethan England, was loyal to the conservative social values of the Elizabethan Era. It is for this reason that Shakespeare portrays Romeo and Juliet's love, going against the morality of honoring parents, social stability, and the conservative value on marriage.

Elizabethan values were heavily influenced by English Puritanism during the time of Shakespeare. Regarding the Puritan values in England, Bayne writes, "The puritan's demand for pure religion and clean living... forced the ordinary man to be moral..." (57). Shakespeare in his play, *Romeo and Juliet*, portrays romantic love, going against the norms of Elizabethan England as causing tragedy. Romeo and Juliet pursued romantic love, which seemed like the most beautiful love on the surface, but Shakespeare shows that their love was fueled by fickle sentimentality and youthful rebellion. Through his conclusion Shakespeare gives the verdict of "death" for such kind of romantic love that goes against the Puritan influenced Elizabethan England value system. One sees that Shakespeare describes of Romeo and Juliet's love as a bad adventure that is pitiful and tragic, and not as a beautiful romantic love.

Like the story of Romeo and Juliet, which condemns romantic love, Korean culture has a strong anti-romantic love trend, and this is due to Korean history. This is shown in the Korean practice of "Joong-Mae" marriage (traditional arranged marriage), whose history began to be recorded during the Yi Dynasty.

"Joong-Mae" marriage is an arranged marriage system, existent during the Yi Dynasty as well as now, in which a third-person intercedes between two families in order to bring to fruition a successful marriage between a daughter of a respected family and a son of a respectable family. In terms of written record, "Joong-Mae" started long before Koryo period but became formalized during Yi Dynasty (1400s-1905). The Confucian way of "Joong-Mae" began to flourish during the Yi Dynasty of Korea, which aggressively encouraged Confucian philosophy. In "Joong-Mae" marriage, fathers would arrange for the marriage of their sons and daughters; children's thoughts on their prospective spouse were not taken into consideration in the process of "Joong-Mae" marriage. "Joong-Mae" consisted of four steps, which are: "Eu-Hon," "Nap-Chae," "Nap-Pye," and "Chin-Young." First, "Eu-Hon" was the process of mediating between the families (Kwon). The two families with a son and a daughter at a proper age for a marriage, which is from sixteen to nineteen, would hire a matchmaker to ask for parents' intention to marry their children, and thus further proceed to reward the marriage.

The first step of "Joong-Mae" marriage was "Goong-Hap," which is the process of predicting the marital harmony as assessed by the fortuneteller. The "Eu-Hon" process would not only include examination of appearances, personality and learning but also family, relatives, and even hereditary diseases. A matchmaker might serve as a messenger between the two, but letters were also commonly used to carry out the "Eu-Hon" process (Kwon).

The next stage, the "Nap-Chae" process was the approval stage of the marriage or more commonly known as engagement. Commonly, the man's family requests marriage from the woman's family, and "Nap-Chae" is the ceremonial process of requesting the approval for marriage. The man's family would send a sculpted wooden goose with the son's fortune written on a paper. Then, the woman's family would choose a proper date for the marriage and send back a paper with the daughter's written fortune (Kwon).

Thirdly, "Nap-Pye" (which followed "Nap-Chae") is the step in which the son's friends, "Hamjin-Abi," carries a box of presents to the woman's family in order to set as evidence and to let the world know that the couple is getting married. It was similar to the process of engagement in a way that they let the town know about their marriage. However, unlike now when "Hamjin-Abi" comes from friends, in the Yi Dynasty

47

period, "Hamjin-Abi" was usually a servant of the family or anyone with acquaintance with the groom. It is a generalized rule for "Nap-Pye" to be done at night (Kwon).

Lastly, "Chin-Young" is the actual marriage ceremony. The groom goes to the bride's house to pick her up and bring her to his house. "Chin-Young" consists of series of ceremonies, including the bride bowing three times and the husband bowing twice to each other, sharing a drink from the same cup, and sleeping in one room. The next morning, the bride formally greets the family and stays at the house for three days. The bride returns to the house until the formal day is set for her to come back. One important fact is that couples with the same last name (such as the man and the woman having "Kim" as the last name before marriage) could not marry. And the man needed to be over 18 and the woman needed to be over 16 to legally marry, but this regulation was often not kept strictly (Kwon).

However, now in the information era, the conventional meaning of "Joong-Mae" has changed. The direct role of matchmakers shifted to family friends and the Internet. For instance, a family friend would introduce the man and the woman to meet and see if they could come to a marriage agreement. Unlike two centuries ago, prospective marriage candidates play a greater role in the decision-making process, and the marriage is not required so hastily after the meeting. Also, the internet plays a big role in aiding "Joong-Mae" in the modern era. From one of the famous Korean search engines, http://naver.com, two hundred and thirty results showed up under the word "Joong-Mae," most of which were business websites introducing one to the opposite sex. Based on one's aptitude, personality, interests, and social economic status, the computer system finds the best match for the wooer. Then, who is known as "a couple manager," or similar to "matchmaker" would call the two adaptable wooers to find out the best time for them to meet. Many people seek to get help from the Internet because it would offer them a chance to meet other people from a broad spectrum of Korean society, socially, geographically, and economically.

Korean society values "Joong-Mae" due to its Confucian influence on the peninsula. For half a millennium, women played no bigger role than supporting the domestic household. There was not much socialization among the adolescents in the Yi Dynasty. Women were not allowed any form of education but simple writing, which would be taught at home by their mothers. Confucianism's basic ideology was to fulfill one's duties, whether it be a king, subjects, or citizens, and maintain the harmony and peace as a nation. So, one had to understand and accept the position, or social class, they were in. Thus, Confucian centric Yi Dynasty enforced respect between man and woman, and love was considered as an embarrassment. Especially, "Nam Nyu Chil Se Boo Dong Suk," a philosophy created in the Yi dynasty, stated that boy and a girl over the age of seven should not be in one place together. As shown, the Confucian society naturally shaped the marriage process and the "Joong-Mae" marriage became a reasonably expected custom to Koreans. Interestingly enough, the sentiment of support for the Korean "Joong-Mae" system seems to find a sympathetic ear in William Shakespeare, who supported the Elizabethan system of arranged marriage by shaping the romantic-love story of Romeo and Juliet as a tragedy.

"SHAKESPEARE'S SUPPORT OF TRADITIONAL ARRANGED MARRIAGE AND THE KOREAN JOONG-MAE SYSTEM"

Bibliography

Bayne, Ronald. "Religion." *Shakespeare's England: An Account of the Life and Manners of His Age*, Vol. I. 1962 ed.

Bloom, Harold. *Shakespeare: The Invention of the Human*. New York: Riverhead Books, 1998.

Brodwin, Leonora. "Aspects of Love." *Shakespeare for Students*. Mark W. Scott. Washington D.C. 1992. 493-498.

Brown, Carolyn E. "Juliet's Taming of Romeo." *Studies in English Literature (Rice)*. 1996.

Literary Reference Center. EBSCOhost. Old Tappan High School Library, Old Tappan, NJ. <http://web.ebscohost.com/lrc/detail?vid=1&hid=102&sid=fd34 bd04-db3e-49bc-8dfe-544a2794e85f%40sessionmgr108>.

Cook, Ann J. "Social Restrictions Against Illicit Unions in Romeo and Juliet" *Readings on Romeo and Juliet*. Bruno Leone. Greenhaven Press, San Diego 1998. 100-2.

Hurh, Won Moo. *The Korean Americans*. Westport: Greenwood Press, 1998.

Kim, Heerak Christian. *Korean-American Youth Identity and 9/11: An Examination of Korean-American Ethnic Identity in Post - 9/11 America*. Highland Park: The Hermit Kingdom Press, 2008.

Kwon, Soon-Hyung. "Was There a Divorce in Chosun Period?" Yung Nam University. Yung Nam University. 1 Oct. 2008 <http://ynucc.yu.ac.kr/~edupht/book/ chosun1/2.htm>.

Lemay, Eric. "Star-Crossed Something-or-Others." *Harvard Review*. 2007. Literary Reference Center. EBSCOhost. Old Tappan High School Library, Old Tappan, NJ. 28 Feb, 2008.

<http://web.ebscohost.com/lrc/detail?vid=1&hid=108&sid=73ee e7de-7d9b-4f8a-820e-9af75f61f38f%40sessionmgr102>.

McKittrick, Ryan. *American Repertory Theatre. Retrieved* March 29, 2008. < http://www.amrep.org/articles/4_3a/romeus.html>.

MacFarlane, Alan. *Marriage and Love in England: Modes of Reproduction 1300-1840.* Blackwell Pub, 1987.

Ros, Maggi. "Marriage and Family." Life in Elizabethan England. Retr. Feb 10, 2008. http://elizabethan.org/compendium/10.html

Stewart, Gail B. *Life in Elizabethan London.* New York: Lucent Books, 2002.

Stone, Lawrence. *The Family, Sex and Marriage in England 1500-1800.* Penguin Books Ltd, 1990.

Van Doren, Mark. "Aspects of Love." *Shakespeare for Students.* Mark W. Scott. Washington D.C. 1992. 493-498.

"Back in Korea: My Best Times"
Jake Byun (Harrington Park Middle School, New Jersey, USA)

When I was born in Korea, my mom didn't take care of me. My grandparents did, until I was 3 years old. My grandparents lived in Jang An Dong. My parents could not take care of me, so that after leaving my grandparents' house, my aunt took care of me for four years, which means until I graduated from kindergarten. After kindergarten, my mom bought me a Digimon card deck.

And I came to live with my parents in Seoul. First grade was the best, because teachers didn't give us much homework. Also, all the work they gave us was so easy. The name of my school was 별말초등학교, but in fourth grade, one huge school was created in front our apartment, and the name of that school was 나눔초등학교. My first school was

52

built really far away, almost about 500 meters away. My second school was located right in front of our apartment.

Second grade was horrible, because we had to memorize multiplication charts, and it was driving me nuts. It took me about three weeks to master it. Third grade was really easy and was the second best. Division was really easy, because I had mastered multiplication. There was nothing hard in third grade. Our teacher let us watch DVD after huge tests. Fourth grade was the worst of all the grades. Teacher gave us too much homework, and too much work. After fourth grade, I came to America, which where I'm staying right now.

Once, in Korea, I went to the middle of the forest with my church friends. My church was located in the forest and it was huge with 700 hundred members. Our church name was 뉴라이프교회 I really don't remember where the forest was, but I still remember my best friend's name. His name was Kim, Sang-Wha. He's family was really rich and they had two cars! In Korea, people usually have only one car at most. We became friends when we became classmates. We were planning to stay in the forest about three days. First day in forest was not fun and boring. All we did was unpack our stuff, eat our lunch, go fishing and stay inside when it rained, and we talked until it was time to eat, and then obviously we fell asleep.

Second day, it was so fun. I woke up at six A.M and went outside for a walk and then I saw a frog on the rock. So I caught it and put it on my friend's face. About two seconds later he opened his eyes slightly, and he freaked out. When he freaked out, he screamed so loud that other friends woke up. After everyone woke up, my friends and other friends went boating. Everyone grabbed their canoe and jump into the river. My friends were splashing each other, and our boats crashed into each other. One of my friends stood up while he was on the canoe and fell off from the canoe. After the boating, we went to the low river with our nets, and ate our lunch. After lunch, we threw our nets into the river. We caught some crayfish, bugs, fish, salamander, and a small tiny baby eel. We saw a lot of beaver marks on trees. We also saw two wild turkeys. We were hoping to see a bear, but we didn't. When we were walking to our cabin (where we slept) one of my friends told us that they saw a snake, but we were too late to see the snake. We took some rest for the pillow fight that night. We ate our dinner around seven P.M.

"Back in Korea: My Best Times"

At seven thirty, we had a campfire. I put my marshmallow on a stick and put a chocolate on the top. It was really hot when I tried to reach the fire with my marshmallow. My face felt like it was just going to burn into ashes. Finally, I made it! With a happy face on my face, I ate the marshmallow. The chocolate I put on the top of the marshmallow melted and became chocolate syrup. It was so good that I was going crazy for another one. I ate three marshmallows, but I wanted more marshmallows. After the campfire, we had a dance party. Everyone was dancing randomly, but my friends and I interrupted them. Also, we got a lot of missions to complete. After the party, we went to our cabin and had another food party, but it was only for our cabin. We were eating cookies, Pusha Pusha, and other snacks. Pusha Pusha is ramen except you spray the powder on the ramen. Friends from another cabin came inside to our cabin and stole our food. After the food party, we had a huge pillow fight. Everyone was hitting each other, but not their own cabin members. We came outside and hit other cabin members. So everyone came out and hit anything that they could hit. After a huge fight, we fell asleep.

Third day was really fun. We got to stay one more night, because of the rain. So we went fishing, but all we caught was fish that were too small to take home. We were yawning incredibly a lot. Suddenly, my friend yelled as if he saw something horrible. We were looking where my friend yelled. There was a dead eel. My other friend asked him why he screamed, and he said he did that to scare us. So, my friends picked up the fish and use it as bait. About 15 minutes later, the fishing rod started to move. It was the rod with eel on it. We pulled the eel together, and we caught a fish about the size of a DVD player, but we let it go because it was illegal to take it home. We had a huge lunch with my friends. After the lunch, we had a paintball war. Everyone got one gun, five packs of paintballs, and a goggle to wear. I was in team B. When the war began, the first thing we did was to go to the cabin and wait until someone came. We were also making plans in the cabin. I got picked to spy on the other team while they were making a plan. I saw one of my friends in team C, so I followed him, but I got busted. It was a good thing that he didn't come close to his team or if he came close to his team, I probably might have died there. I ran quickly to our cabin and hid myself. We heard a loud noise outside. The spy came, and he told us that team A and team C were having a huge fight. So we attacked the back side of team C, because they were losing horribly. So team C was dying and we ran away when team C ran away. When it was dark, everyone took a shower and had dinner. After the dinner, all of my friends came to the place where we ate. We saw an old man with a big case. He grabbed something and showed us. It was a bird, but it couldn't fly because the old man had taken out the important feather from the bird. That night, he brought so many different animals you can't usually see. My favorite animal was a weasel; it was the best of all. At that night, I thought I was at the zoo.

Next morning, I woke up at six again. My usual time when I wake up is six. First, we ate our first breakfast. I had no idea why we didn't eat our breakfast, everyday. After breakfast, I had some Mychew from my friend. Mychew is a Korean gum. The yogurt flavor is the best of all the flavors from Mychew. When I came out, my friends were playing some kind of a game called Dragonball. Dragon ball is a game anywhere you can play, but it is really hard to explain, because you have to know a lot of skills with which you can attack the opponent. My favorite Korean game is Chopstick. I'm not sure if it's a Korean game.

Chopstick is a kind of math and thinking game. How you play is first, you have one finger up both hands and if the opponent hits you with a left hand finger then your left hand has to raise another finger, but if your fingers are all up in left or right hand then that hand is out. So, it was our last day to in the forest. I was packing up my stuff. My stupid bag didn't fit every stuff that I had brought. The bus came, and we went inside the bus. We arrived at home while watching DVD on the bus. That was one of my best weeks ever in Korea .

Another time, I went to Everland during summer vacation with my family for a week. My father's name is Byun, Hoon, and he is the bravest and highest family member in our family. My mother's name is Park, Kyoung-Sook. She is really nice to me, but she cares too much…but she is the best! I have two sisters in our family: one of my sisters is named Byun, Young Woo and my youngest sister's name is Byun, Sun Woo. They have same characteristics, but Jodie (Byun, Sun Woo) is more greedy. It took us one hour to arrive there with our car from Seoul to Yongin. First day, we went to Everland. When we got there, there were some courses to go on. We went to the animal zoo, first. We saw a lot of wild animals in there.

There was a huge giant bear standing at the middle of the animal zoo. We went inside there, to check out what was in the tree. When we went in there, I saw some posters about the bear show. Bear show started at two P.M and closed at five P.M. So, we went inside. They gave information paper to us. There was a curtain which screened off the stage. Suddenly, it opened, and the bear went inside the water. If you want to know the rest, then visit Everland in Yongin, but remember it is in Korea. Second day, we planned to ride some roller coasters. My sister was obviously scared and I enjoyed that very much. I also rode the rollercoaster that goes up very high and falls down very fast. One guy's shoes fell off, so the worker picked it up and gave it to him. I also rode Viking. Viking is a pirate looking ship that swings really high back and forward. It was so fun. I sat at the seat where it was really scary, but it was fun.

Third day, I went to the zoo again, but this time, I went to the aquarium. I saw a lot of sharks. I even gave them food. Of course, I touched them. It felt like a slippery skin, and slippery as soap. I also saw a sea turtle. My sister really enjoyed touching crocodile for some reason. Well, I didn't, because it felt like a not-so-smooth rock. I wondered if I

56

could see a huge whale. I wish I can see a giant squid once in my lifetime. Fourth day, I went to Caribbean bay.

Caribbean bay is a gigantic swimming course. I just love that place, especially during summer. During summer, when you go to the Caribbean bay, they let us go outside and play with more fun stuff, but in winter, fall, and spring they don't let us go outside. There is a huge wave pool in Caribbean bay, but it's for summer only. Every time the horn beeps loud the huge wave comes. When I was a kid I went there with my jacket on so that I could float on the water, but that doesn't mean I can't swim. I went to the scariest ride with my father and it was really fun for me, but my father got scared a little bit. I ran to my mom for ice cream, but she just hates ice cream; it is so weird how she hates it. After the scary ride, I and my father went to the kid's corner. My sister was playing as if she were drinking a beer. At the end of the day, she actually bought me the ice cream.

In Korea, I also had tae kwon do field trips with my master and my friends. First, we had sliding party at the do-jo (tae kwon do room); we had to wear swimming suit then we just ran and then slid on our belly. It was really slippery so that I just fell down every time I stood up. Second, we played dodge ball, I wasn't really good at it, but at least now I'm good at it. The older brothers threw so hard that many people got hurt. Third, we watched a movie. We watched *Chronicles of Narnia*. Fourth, we watched scary a movie. I and my friends didn't sleep until six A.M. In the morning, we played games and ate ramen. Some people ate three! I only ate one, but I still had a good time. We were playing games after the eating; we asked our master for coins and then game was on! The one with the fighting was the most popular game. Every week, games changed to different games. I still miss that tae kwon do place.

Another time, we had a huge sleep over. It was at my friend's house, and we had so much fun. My friend's name is Kim, Sang Wha, who is my best friend in Church. First, we had nothing to do, so we played games. Suddenly, one guy told us to have a competition on, and I basically won. At night, one of my friends was sick so I slept next to him, and we got to sleep in the other room. My friend passed me over some books to read. So we didn't fall asleep. After my friend's parents fell asleep, we went down to the computer room. We were playing computer games like crazy. At five A.M, we switched places. Now, I was playing computer games like crazy like my friend had. My friend went up stairs and brought birthday boy there, so he woke up and we switched places. When it was seven A.M, other friends came down and complained about why we didn't tell them about it. I said that the other friend made us do it. After that speech, everyone stared at him. He said that the guys were too heavy, but the thing is that the birthday boy was the heaviest person. So he got hit by our friends. We ate fries, chicken, potato fries, and other fast food. It was my first breakfast with fast food. I mean, who eats fast food for breakfast?

We played more games and my friends' eyes turned to mine too. Both of us were going crazy with games. So I slept a little bit and drank some water. After that, I returned to normal.

You see I had a lot of stories in my life, but I'm still going to keep building until I die. Probably, I might get more good stories in my life. As I keep growing up. I'll try to get more stories that are true in my life and have a life that is memorable. I wish I can go back to Korea or go back in time so we experience what we did, again.

"My Korean Family"

Sora Yang (Baulkham Hills Selective High School, AUSTRALIA)

Our metaphorical first step on Australia:

1st of July, 1993.
It's a cold winter's morning, at the airport.
Two people. A young couple. The student and his wife.
Two suitcases – all their belongings.
Don't forget the nappy bag – for the little girl strapped on the young woman's back.

Family Member No.1: My father.
While he can be somewhat strict and severe, paradoxically, he has a quirky sense of humour, and is generally good-humoured. It's what I like best about him – his sense of humour, he can almost always make me

60

laugh, even when I'm in the very depths of self-induced despair. There's not much I don't like about my father, and I'm immensely proud of him.

In retrospect, now that I'm older, I can appreciate the difficulty of the circumstances, and my father's perseverance in overcoming those difficulties – language difficulties, economic hardships, and uncertainty. It can't have been easy – toiling away as a humble student in Australia when he had graduated from the prestigious Seoul National University in Korea. Although he doesn't say much about it, upon reflection, to me, it's inspiring. Despite everything, he persisted, overcoming hardships to achieve *his* goals, not just taking the easy road. The knowledge of his experiences has helped me to dream of *my* own goal– to aspire to be the best that I can, in every way, to persevere despite the circumstances to achieve my dreams.

Family Member No.2: My mother.
Ever supportive, understanding and patient. She's lenient without being lax, tolerant but firm, and passionate about our education – I remember being read two books, every night, one in Korean, and one in English. Looking back, I can see that my mother encouraged my love of reading from an early age. She's also the person who taught me the importance of education, my mother was my personal tutor, those hours spent pouring over workbooks and homework have paid off... Not only this, my mother is the person who endeavored to help us understand the importance of learning Korean – sending an unwilling child (who questioned the need of learning a second language) to an additional day of language school wouldn't have been easy – but she persisted, until I came to realize the importance of culture, heritage, and national pride – because you can't forsake your nationality, and what it represents, even if you wanted to. I believe that language is an expression of the culture of a country, and being able to speak, read, and write Korean is my way of being in touch with my national and cultural heritage of Korea. Because no matter where I live, and what other languages I can speak, I am Korean.

Family Member No.4: My first sibling, first younger sister.
Sori Yang was born good natured, now known by Sally; she's in her first year of high school. Almost four years younger than myself, Sally is well-meaning and affable, easily amused. While I regard her as a

61

younger sister who needs to be looked after, rather than a friend to confide in, she's been a constant companion as far back as I can remember. Back when all of my schoolmates were Caucasian, and I was the only Asian, let alone Korean, my sister was the only person I knew of who went through the same experiences as me – the only one on my side of the cultural schism that separated me from everyone else I knew. While I've graduated from Saturday Korean School, my sister still attends, and is much involved in extra-curricular activities held at the school – the Drama Club, the Band (she plays the flute), and now is practicing for a Dance Performance with her classmates for the school's yearly presentation.

Family Member No.5: My second sibling, and second younger sister.
Known as Skye to the non-Korean population, she's currently in her second year of primary school. A younger sister by 10 years, Skye is sweet-natured, and still very much a kid. Now in her second year of school, I've seen her struggle to adjust to school life; trying to learn English as well as Korean. Her difficulties in adapting to school life reminded me of the hardships of language and cultural barriers, but her eventual adjustment and happiness in attending school brought to light the consistent effort and patience needed to overcome these difficulties, and that in the end, things did turn out alright.

Family Member No.6: My third sibling, and one and only younger brother.
Last, but definitely not the least, Jeong-Hun Yang was born puckish, on the 19th of August 2004. He responds to either Jeong-Hun or Jonathan, depending on his mood, and is currently occupied with pre-school and wreaking havoc wherever and whenever possible, and begging forgiveness in the most irresistibly penitent way possible. Mischievous and happy-go-lucky, Jeong-Hun, at the tender age of four, is already a bilingual. Watching him pick up English as fast as Korean, even preferring English to Korean at times reminds me not to take what I have for granted, and the need for consistent and constant use of Korean to prevent my knowledge and development from deteriorating.

7th of October, 2008.
It's a warm spring evening, at a house in the suburbs.

Two people. A middle aged couple. The lecturer and his wife.
Their house, full of furnishings – everything that's been acquired over the years.
Don't forget the big yard with the see-saw – for the two children squealing with laughter, and the two teenaged girls, the younger one scolding, the other smiling as she watches them play.

It's been 15 years, 3 months and 6 days since the Yang family came to Australia.

Bigger. Better.
We're still here.

"Back in Time to Lewis and Clark Expedition"

Paul Sungbae Park (Northern Valley Regional
High School, Old Tappan, New Jersey, USA)

My Name is George White, and I am a child of a Revolutionary War veteran, who was proud to fight for his country. I guess that is why I grew up with patriotism, and wanted to participate in the history-making of the United States the same way my father did. I was born towards the end of the Revolutionary war in Philadelphia, when my mother was worrying about the safety of my father fighting in the war. Her constant worrying about my father drew her to be more religious. She made sure that I was raised a strict Presbyterian; I went to the Presbyterian Church in the center of town with my mother every Sunday. After my father came back, he seemed to have become much more religious as well. He said, " 'Tis grace that saved me from death." My father worked as a baker near the church. He tried to get me educated like "the nice middle class folk," who wore a nice suit to church.

But, because my father worked as a local baker, and my family was working class, I was not academically prepared enough to be accepted to West Point Military Academy. So, I started to work with my father at the bakery for his boss. But, after hearing constant war stories as I worked side by side with my father, my desire for the history-making of the United States was reawakened, and I enlisted in the U.S. Military. Like my father, I started at the bottom of the military rank, as a private. In 1802, I was enlisted into the First U.S. Infantry at age nineteen. After serving in the army for two years, I have learned that no military glory would come from the tough repetitive military life; so, I eagerly joined the Corps of Discovery when Captain Lewis recruited volunteers for the expedition into the Louisiana Territory (White).

After taking first steps towards exciting participation in the history-making of the United States by joining the Crops of Discovery, I wanted to find out more information about the leader of the expedition. So, I voraciously read the latest newspapers, and found out much about Captain Lewis. Captain Lewis's significance for the expedition started with the Louisiana Purchase. In 1801, Jefferson was elected the President of the United States, in the midst of divisions and problems arising from prolonged wars with foreign nations and conflict with the Indians. Thus, the colonies "had no fondness for foreigners of any kind, but a fact that could not be avoided was the fact that whichever nation controlled the mouth of the Mississippi River controlled the whole Mississippi Valley" (Chidsey, *Louisiana* 115). Although that nation was Spain at the time shortly before the election of Jefferson, the ownership of that area connecting with the Mississippi River soon changed. In April 30, 1800, Treaty of San Ildefonso was signed to give the Louisiana Territory back to France. However, the Louisiana Territory was soon purchased by the U.S.

President Jefferson picked James Monroe to make the trip to France for the purchase of New Orleans and its islands and, perhaps, Florida. However, Livingston, U.S. minister to France who was supposedly in France before Monroe reached France negotiated with the French foreign minister, Talleyrand. Napoleon had been economically suffering from the Haitian rebellion, so Talleyrand offered to sell the whole Louisiana Territory for twenty-three million dollars. Livingston knowing that Monroe would take all the credit if he came, decided to buy the land in April 30th, 1803. The news reached America on June 30, and most of the citizens seemed to find it exhilarating to be rich in land. But Livingston, a Republican, made the deal so the Federalists wanted to embarrass Livingston. The Federalists stated that "it was a payment for a vast wasteland nobody knows anything about, and it represents $3 for every man, woman, and child in the whole country" (Chidsey, *Louisiana* 144). However, all Jefferson worried about was whether U.S. could buy Louisiana and what should be done after it was bought, whether it should be sold or used for some other purposes. He worried especially about the rights of the Indians in the territory and how many Indians there were. Another worry that President Jefferson had was that the constitution did not give the President the right to buy foreign properties, so he framed an amendment after the purchase. Senate voted twenty-four to seven, and the Purchase treaty was ratified in 1803 (Chidsey, *Louisiana* 153-4).

Louisiana Territory became a splendid prize for the Americans. America now was in a strategic position in control of the mouth of the Mississippi, which also provided an escape route from the British blockade. Besides the military benefits, there were economic benefits as well. The land could provide cotton, sugar, and tobacco worth 20 million dollars just in the New Orleans area. The Louisiana Territory was a huge landmass of 828,000 square miles that doubled the size of our country (Chidsey, *Louisiana* 166).

After the Purchase, President Jefferson commissioned Meriwether Lewis to explore the new territory. Jefferson instructed Lewis, giving him specific details regarding preparation of the journey, and also to communication and trade with the Indians during the journey. Another aspect of Lewis's duty for the expedition was to "explore the Missouri river, and such principal stream of it, as, by tis course and communication with the waters of the Pacific by its course and communication with the waters of the Pacific Ocean, offer the most direct and practicable water communication across the continent, for the purposes of commerce" (Jefferson). To facilitate mapping Louisiana Territory for trade and travel, President Jefferson demanded keeping specific details. Thus, President Jefferson said, "Beginning at the mouth of the Missouri, you will take observations of latitude and longitude, at all remarkable points on the river, and especially at the mouths of rivers, at rapids, at islands, and other places and objects distinguished by such natural marks..." (Jefferson). Furthermore, President Jefferson demanded that Lewis keep a journal; Jefferson instructed, "Your observations are to be taken with great pains and accuracy; to be entered distinctly and intelligibly for others as well as yourself" (Jefferson).

Meriwether Lewis, President Jefferson's personal secretary, was born in Virginia on August 18th, 1774. Lewis was a son of a planter who died fighting in the Revolutionary War when Lewis was only five. At age eighteen, he eagerly volunteered for Jefferson's Michaux expedition, but Jefferson turned him down saying that he was too young. Instead, Lewis joined the regular army on the frontiers of western Pennsylvania and Ohio, and "made a name for himself as a promising officer before Jefferson brought him to Washington in 1801" (Duncan 9). During his military service, Lewis served under William Clark, who was his commanding officer (Holloway 20). After his military service under Clark ended, Lewis then moved to the White House where he set up residence in the East Room of the White House. There, he copied presidential documents, ran errands, and drew up a list of army commanders who could be expected to be loyal to the new administration (Snyder 15). During his two years of service to President Jefferson, Lewis intimately became acquainted with Jefferson's "interests in the West-its geography, its plants and animals, its people and their habitats, and its potential for settlers" (Duncan 9). So, it is understandable that in June of 1803, President Jefferson chose Lewis, his trusted personal secretary, as the captain of the journey into the western Louisiana Territory.

After being commissioned by President Jefferson, Meriwether Lewis chose his former commanding officer and friend, William Clark, to be the co-leader of the expedition. However, the reply from Clark did not come right away, and Lewis chose a back up, who was Lt. Moses Hooke. However, Clark sent a late reply three days later, writing that, "This is an undertaking fraited with many difeculties, but My friend I do assure you that no man lives with whome I would perfur to undertake Such a Trip" (Snyder 15). After receiving an affirmative reply, Lewis decided that he would lead the Louisiana expedition with Clark and not with Lt. Hooke. To Jefferson, only one person was the supreme commander, but "Lewis could not bear to see his former commanding officer as a subordinate and offered Clark an equal role" (Snyder 15). So, Lewis sent a letter to the Congress requesting that Clark be a co-leader of the expedition. President Jefferson accepted the request, so for the duration of the expedition, the two leaders would be called Captain Lewis and Captain Clark (Snyder 16).

After the leadership of the Louisiana expedition was formalized, Lewis then began the preparation in August 1803. In Philadelphia, he spent $2,160.41, out of the $2,500 given by the Congress on ammunition, firearms, as well as supplies including clothing, pliers, chisels, hatchets, "12 pounds of soap, 194 pounds of 'portable soup'..." and other navigational instruments necessary for the journey (Duncan 10-11). Lewis then went over to Pittsburgh where he waited for three keelboats that were being built. They were "55-foot-long keelboats [that] could be rowed, sailed, pushed, or pulled." It held "12 tons and 22 men -two captains and 20 oarsman" (Duncan 41). Lewis took the expedition very seriously, so, he prepared excessively for it. Before the expedition, Lewis learned from four scientists at the University of Pennsylvania. Dr. Benjamin Rush, nation's most esteemed physician, "assembled a medical kit for the explorer and lectured him on its uses" (Duncan 10). Also, Benjamin Barton instructed Lewis on how to describe and preserve botanical specimens, and Robert Patterson taught Lewis how to determine latitude and longitude. Casper Wistar showed Lewis how to search for signs of ancient beasts, using fossils (Duncan 9-10). After all the preparation, on August 31, 1803, Lewis and his Corps of Volunteers for Northwestern Discovery, including me, moved from Pittsburgh down the Ohio River to pick up Clark who came with his slave York and several other recruits.

York was Captain Clark's African American slave born in about 1770, roughly the same age as Clark. In Virginia, where Clark grew up, it wasn't uncommon for a boy to have a body servant from among his former playmates (Betts 84). Growing up in the Northern Upper South, York could do much more than just pick cotton. He was a hunter and could provide basic nurse services in times of emergency because he was knowledgeable in frontier herbal medicine (Betts 19-24). On many occasions, the Indians were fascinated by York's dark skin. Few scrubbed his skin to see if it was real, and some examined him from "top to toe," according to Sergeant Ordway (Betts 16). When he met the Arikara Indians of South Dakota, he told a joke to the Indians that he had been a wild animal until caught and tamed by his master. I thought this was very amusing; York was the "wag and the wit of the expedition… keeping us in laughter from beginning to end of the expedition" (Betts 18).

When I met some of the crew of Corps of Discovery at Camp Dubois, not all of the crew were soldiers (Duncan 21). The members of the Corps of Discovery were forty-five, which consisted of "nine young men from Kentucky, fourteen soldiers of the United States army who volunteered their services, and two French guides, and York, Captain Clark's slave" (Lewis, *Expedition* 1:2). Many had different talents to the odyssey; some were "woodsmen, hunters, carpenters, cooks, boatwrights, and gunsmiths" (Snyder 34). All of us were very healthy and "around six feet tall, broad-shouldered, with the grace of a natural athlete" (Ambrose, *Lewis* 42).

There were twenty-seven unmarried soldiers out of the forty-five crews. The youngest of the group was George Shannon who was eighteen (Ambrose, *Lewis* 42), and the oldest of the group was Private Patrick Gass who was thirty-two (Snyder 35). Whenever the captains were absent, Sergeant John Ordway took command. Lewis assigned each sergeant duties on the keelboat. These jobs included steering the boat, arranging baggage, attending to the compass, commanding the guard, managing the sails, and seeing that the men at their oars do their duty (Snyder 40). The sergeants rotated the duties; each sergeant oversaw eight crews.

The expedition reached St. Louis in Illinois Country in December of 1803. There, the Corps of Discovery set up a base of operations called Camp Dubois near Wood River close to St. Louis (Snyder 33). At the camp, Captain Clark ordered his men to have a "true respect for their own Dignity," meaning to behave in an orderly manner regarding the fact that they are a military group visiting a town with many people (Snyder 36). However, when the captains were absent and Sgt. Ordway was in charge, three privates, Collins, Hall, and Werner, were "absent without leave after one of the parties in town" (Duncan 29). Clark was furious, and he wrote in his journal, "a fine Day 3 men Confined for misconduct, I had a Court martial and punishment" (Lewis, *Journals* 1). Clark set up a court, consisting of five members, including Captain Lewis and other sergeants, which made judicial decisions to prove one's guilt or innocence. Private Collins received fifty lashes as a punishment, and Werner and Hall each faced twenty-five lashes (Snyder 36).

Captain Lewis had spent most of the winter in St. Louis sending specimens back to President Jefferson, and Captain Clark, most of the winter in Camp Dubois, building the fort and training the men. During the winter, we picked up few more canoes and double-checked our supplies. Finally, on May 14th, 1804, we traveled northwest, up the Missouri River (Ambrose, *Lewis* 45). On board, Captain Clark instructed us to keep a journal. I decided to, but since I had never written one before, I peeked over at Joseph Whitehouse's Journal to see what a journal entry looked like. Whitehouse was another private who kept a journal, and he wrote in his journal, "The men hoisted Sail and Set out in high Spirits for the western Expedition" (Snyder 35).

"Back in Time to Lewis and Clark Expedition"

Second day out of Camp Dubois, Captain Lewis walked around the town alone. We tried to accompany him, but he told us that he appreciated thinking in solitude (Snyder 37). I was not surprised because Captain Lewis had much more to think about, including the scientific description of the territory, the administration of the crew, and the safety and success of the expedition. In contrast, we were focused on adventure and experiencing New Territory, but Captain Lewis outlined that our first destination was the Mandan Indians. The Corps of Discovery faced many difficulties on the way to the Mandan Indians, our destination for the winter camp of 1804. The Corps of Discovery was traveling against the current, so it required the crew rowing strenuously. Also, the water was muddy and the temperature was moist and hot, adding to our difficulty in rowing (Snyder 42). I could not stand the heat, wearing a military uniform (White). However, the biggest problem was insects; Clark wrote on June 17th, "The Ticks and Musquiters are verry troublesom" (Lewis, *Journals* 13). Discipline of the members of the crew became another major problem on June 28-29th, 1804. Private John Collins became drunk while on duty, guarding the whiskeys (Ambrose, *Undaunted* 148). He was punished with hundred lashes oh his bareback. The hundred lashes were divided into twenty five lashes for four consecutive days (Snyder 44) because Captain Clark did not want him dead; despite private Collins's disciplinary problem, the Lewis and Clark Expedition needed John Collins. I personally think he deserved the punishment; the expedition would continue for at least another year, and if all of us were not in order, we might become endangered as a group.

Early August of 1804, our expedition arrived at the mouth of Platte River. We inferred that Indians resided in the area because a domesticated dog belonging to Indians was walking along the bank. Encouraged, Lewis and Clark pushed ahead with the main tasks of the expedition, as instructed by President Jefferson: "Show the flag and open trade negotiations with the Indians" (Jefferson). Although we have not yet reached the Mandan territory, Lewis and Clark decided to meet Indians of Otto and Missouri nations headed by three chiefs from each nation (Ambrose, *Undaunted* 154). Captain Lewis first made a lengthy speech consisting of 2,500 words, which was about half an hour long, and a French guide translated Captain Lewis's speech into an Indian dialect. In his speech Captain Clark tried to persuade him that the "Great White

70

Father," referring to President Jefferson, who would give them protection, so they should trade with the U.S. (Ambrose, *Undaunted* 156).

Since I could not understand French or Otto, I had no idea of finding out if Captain Lewis's speech was translated accurately or if Indians understood what was implied. In the end, all the Indians wanted was a trade, especially for guns to fight their enemies, the Omahas (Holloway 37). The Captains distributed to the Indians some presents, which were a breechclout, a bit of paint, and a small medal with President Jefferson's picture on it. Lewis and Clark wanted to save the presents allotted for the Indians and provisions for the trip because there was a long journey in front of them, and they were going to meet many more Indians along the way. So, Lewis only gave a few presents to the Ottos (Ambrose, *Undaunted* 158). After giving the gifts, we continued on with our journey.

During the trip to Mandan Indians, medical problems were another serious obstacle. Sergeant Floyd's condition became worse and worse; "nothing will Stay a moment on his Stomach or bowels" (Lewis, *Journals* 34). Captain Lewis diagnosed it as "Biliose Chorlick," which is a disease showing the symptoms of vomiting, losing appetite, and nasal pain (Ambrose, *Undaunted* 160). On August 1804, sergeant Floyd died from unknown gut pain; he has said the day before he died, "I am going away. I want you to write me a letter" (Lewis, *Expedition* 34). In present day Iowa, the funeral ceremony took place; Lewis read the funeral service, and Clark provided the epitaph. Although "Lewis had shared interest in herb remedies and Clark knew how to set broken bones, remove bullets and treat a wide range of diseases," they were not surgeons or doctors. Modern physicians believe that it was ruptured appendix, which was impossible to cure at the time (Snyder 70). To take sergeant Floyd's position, Private Gass from Pennsylvania was elected as a Sergeant (Ambrose, *Undaunted* 161). All of us were under the sense of despondency; Gass said, "Here Sergeant Floyd died, notwithstanding every possible effort was made by the commanding officers, and other persons, to save his life (Lewis, *Expedition* 35).

Despite the hardships, the journey continued on, and Captain Lewis spent a lot of time in August of 1804, observing and describing different animals and plants. For instance, on August 5th, Lewis killed a bull snake and measured its length and the number of "scuta on its belly and tail, its color, spots, and other distinctive markings" (Ambrose,

Undaunted 153). In order to examine the animals, Lewis always killed the animals and collected specimen. One time on August 12th, 1804, Lewis took twelve soldiers to the lake and caught "490 catfish and upward of three hundred fish of nine other species" (Ambrose, *Undaunted* 153). In the same manner, we were very careful about collecting specimens and unfamiliar species including jackrabbit, antelope, mule deer, and coyote. We also kept records of the botanical species we observed. We have "collected, pressed, and returned with more than 240 plant specimens, which later scientists drew and named" (Duncan 39). Out of the specimens sent to President Jefferson were sixty-seven samples of soil and minerals, Arikara Indian corn, and coils of Indian tobacco (Duncan 85). Indians ate all the plants except ragged robin, but they did not like the taste of any of them (Duncan 39).

Along of the biological and botanical descriptions of the area, our expedition reached the destination with the Mandan Indians on October 25th, 1804 (Duncan 73). We were supposed to spend the winter few hundred miles upstream, but frequent councils with Indians delayed us thirty-seven days (Snyder 89). To spend the winter, we have set up a fort across from the Mandan village called Fort Mandan; we stayed at the fort for five months (Duncan 74). As we began to settle, visitors arrived. One of these was French Canadian trader named Toussaint Charbonneau. He was forty-seven years old when we met him. He worked for the North West Company as a fur trader with the Hidatsas (Ambrose, *Lewis* 74-75). However, his attendance was more appreciated by the presence of his sixteen-year-old wife, Sacajawea, who came from the royal family of the Shoshone Indians (Holloway 67). She had been kidnapped by the Hidatsas Indians at age eleven. There, Charbonneau bought Sacajawea at age 12. The captains decided to take her thinking that it would be an advantage of having a Shoshone-speaking member of the expedition (Holloway 67). We quickly built a fort near the Mandan village. Captain Lewis and Captain Clark shared a single cabin, and the rest of the men were in the other seven (Snyder 91). The cabins were seven feet off the ground to keep away as much coldness as possible, and the roofs were sloped to block out the snow (Duncan 89). The weather was always below zero, so we had to wear layer upon layer of winter clothing to survive (Chidsey, *Lewis* 81). Soon, the snow thawed, and we continued on our expedition.

On April 7th, not all of the crews could continue on their expedition to the Pacific, however. Captain Lewis sent six privates under the leadership of Corporal Warfington to return on eight canoes to the East Coast with President Jefferson's specimens and three French traders to deliver the notes and specimens (Chidsey, *Lewis* 85). I did not go back, but continued to travel up the Missouri River and westward into the area. On April 7th, 1805, thirty-three men including Captain Lewis and Clark along with the rest of the crew and Sacajawea started to sail (Ambrose, *Undaunted* 213). After a few days upstream, we passed beyond the mouth of the Yellowstone, which was filled with wildlife including, "Great numbers of Buffalo, Elk, Deer, antelope, beaver, Porcupines, and water fowls seen to day" (Lewis, *Journals* 104). Animals were not always pleasant and marvelous. One time, a large brown bear attacked us, and one of the hunters finally shot him in the head (Snyder 113).

Despite such difficulties with the animals, we continued to travel through the Missouri River, and finally reached the Shoshone country on August 17, 1805. The Shoshone Indians were hunters as well as gatherers. Their major food source was antelope, salmon, and different berries (Lewis, *Expedition* 365-6). Although they altruistically shared their food with us and were very friendly, they were not good warriors. On one encounter, the warriors armed themselves with bows, arrows, and shields when they heard of the Pahkee warriors approaching. The Shoshone warriors were defeated, and twenty warriors were either killed or made prisoners. So, as a result, "they lost their whole camp except the leathern lodge which they had fitted for us" (Lewis, *Expedition* 367). So, we were obliged to live in huts made with willow brush; "the music and dancing which was in no respect…continued nearly all night" (Lewis, *Expedition* 368).

The captains "called on Sacajawea to interpret at a council" (Snyder 137). Surprisingly enough, the chief was Sacajawea's brother Cameahwait. Chief Cameahwait was in full support, and we bought twenty-nine horses and one mule to travel through the Rocky Mountains with a barter trade of uniforms, rifles, powder, pistol balls, and a pistol, which in total was worth less than twenty dollars (Duncan 139). So, we got better end of the deal. I felt a little bad because Captain Lewis and Clark cheated the brother of the member of our expedition. On August 30th, 1805, we began our journey through the Rockies with Sacajawea,

Toby, a Shoshone Indian whose service as a guide was rented from Chief Cameahwait, and three of his sons.

Our travel was under intense summer heat, so several horses slipped down to the steep, craggy hillsides. "A few were so badly crippled but we could no longer carry a load, but none died" (Holloway 134-5). However, it was not just the horses that left; two of Toby's sons gave up along the way and returned home. On September 9th, 1805, we encountered Flathead Indians at Ross's Hole bought thirteen more horses (Chidsey, *Lewis* 122). Nevertheless, we continued on to find a passage through the gap in the Bitterroot Mountains called the "Lost Trail Pass," in what is today's Idaho (Holloway 135). This passage way was worse than anything that we have encountered previously. As we climbed up and up, the trees became thicker and straighter and the temperature became extremely cold, and its needles of menacing spruce kept poking us as we traveled up (Snyder 139). Now, it was scarcer to find food, so we killed the horses to feed ourselves (Ambrose, *Lewis* 142). The journey through the Bitterroot Mountains continued on for a month from early September to October 9th, 1805.

Once we descended the Bitterroot Mountains, we met the Nez Perces Indians near Columbia River. From their altruistic actions of providing us with buffalo meat, dried salmon, and other foods, I had to conclude that they were friendly people; they saved the crew and me from nearly starving (Snyder 140). On the way to the Nez Perces Indians, we had to survive eating horses and portable soup, so to be provided with such food gave me a great sense of gratitude (Ambrose, *Undaunted* 297-8).

I could not appreciate the comfort for long. Captain Lewis soon made the decision to leave again for the Columbia River. October 11th, 1805, we proceeded through for Columbia River in canoes provided by the Nez Perces. We met another band of Nez Perces Indians about six miles from the camp, where we stayed yesterday. We "were so fortunate as to purchase seven dogs and all the fish they would spare" (Lewis, *Expedition* 2:1-2). One of their peculiar practices was taking off a vapor bath in a special form, I have never seen before. The Indian men carried heated stones into a room formed in the riverbank. There, they poured water on the stones until the steam created a suitable temperature for their purposes. The oddest part of the Nez Perces Indian bath was that the men always took a friend with them, and it was considered one of the

74

highest indignities to refuse to go (Lewis, *Expedition* 2:2). In that region, it seemed as if these baths took place at every bank of Columbia Rivers. "On passing the encampment we passed two more rapids, and some swift water" (Lewis, *Expedition* 2:2-3). Some of the rapids were too dangerous that we almost risked our lives; one of the canoes barely escaped the narrow stream.

On our way down on the Columbia River, we encountered the Sokulk tribe. They "seemed to be of a mild and peaceable disposition, and live in a state of comparative happiness" (Lewis, *Expedition* 2:13). They consumed fish and antelopes for their primary food source. Another fact we have noticed was that all these Indians had soreness of the eyes, as well as deprivation of one of the eyes or both of the eyes. Our crew reasoned that it was due "to the constant reflection of the sun on the waters where they are constantly fishing" (Lewis, *Expedition* 2:13-4). The Sokulks also have very bad teeth in general, which might potentially have resulted from their way of eating salmon. They ate their fish dried, but it was only warmed and not prepared, meaning the scales and rind were consumed along with the flesh (Lewis, *Expedition* 2:14).

We continued on with our journey on Columbia River, and we had to face several heavy tides that almost threatened our lives. After a month of rowing, the Columbia River widened, and the rapids began to worsen, having a tide about three feet. So, Captain Lewis made a decision, "we now examined the rapid below more particularly, and the danger appearing to be too great for the loaded canoes, all those who could not swim were sent with the baggage by land" (Lewis, *Journals* 234). The boat felt like it was going to tip off, and I soon started to regret enlisting for the trip. However, the remorse dissipated on November 7th, 1805, when the fog cleared and disclosed a very wide Pacific Ocean, at the mouth of the Columbia River. Even Captain Clark seemed content; he wrote in his journal, "Ocian in view! O! the joy" (Lewis, *Journals* 264).

With the glorious view of the Pacific Ocean in front of us, we had to vote whether to settle on south of the Columbia River or north of it. We all voted including, York, a slave, and Sacajawea, an Indian woman. So, we were democratic in our voting practices. South of Columbia River won. Thus, we set up a winter fort called Fort Clatsop south of the Columbia River (Holloway 153). The fort consisted of cramped wooden buildings surrounded by wooden barracks. After setting up the fort, we spent the winter gathering supplies for the return trip. We during the winter hunted numerous animals including one hundred and thirty-one elk and twenty deer for food; we also extracted salt from the seawater to use on our food (Holloway 158-9). Some "busied themselves sewing moccasins-exactly 338 pairs, according to Patrick Gass (Duncan 171).

Captain Clark set out to find a place for making salt. On December 15th, 1805, "Captain Clark with sixteen men set out in three canoes, and having rowed for three miles up the river turned up a large creek from the right, and after going three miles further landed about the height of the tide water" (Lewis, *Expedition* 2:97). From the 16th to the 23rd, the settlement was filled with precipitation including rain, snow, and hail (Snyder 171). Lewis noted, "As if it were impossible to have twenty four hours of pleasant weather, the sky last evening clouded, and the rain began and continued through the day" (Lewis, *Expedition* 2:102). At the camp, although it was cold, I think I recovered from my fatigue. On 22nd March of 1806, we left Fort Clatsop and abandoned the canoes there in order to travel lighter.

After months of travel, I was just anxious to get back home. We reached Traveler's Rest in Montana on June 29th, 1806. Captain Lewis and Captain Clark decided to separate and meet up at Yellowstone. Captain Clark followed the same trail of 1805, but Captain Lewis traveled the east to the Great Falls of Missouri in order to look for a short cut and also to find a route into the fur country of Canada (Duncan 207). On July 3rd, 1806, the captains went two separate ways.

I accompanied Captain Lewis, but there were no incidents, except one encounter with a bear. A grizzly bear caused "McNeal's horse to bolt and throw its rider. McNeal whacked the bear over the head with the rifle, and clambered up a nearby willow tree until the bear wandered off" (Snyder 192). From what I heard from other privates, Captain Clark had a rough trip. Only after four days of travel did they find a dugout near Columbus, Montana, and twenty-four of their fifty horses, which were stolen by Crow Indians. So, twenty men, Sacagawea, and fifty horses suffered along with Captain Clark. After crossing the Continental Divide, Captain Clark's team reclaimed their cache at Three Forks, which our combined party tied together last year to lighten our load (Snyder 193).

PAUL SUNGBAE PARK

On August 12th, 1806, we reunited with Captain Clark. However, a day earlier, Cruzatte, a private who is blind in one eye, shot Captain Lewis on the thigh thinking that it was an elk (Snyder 194). Surprisingly, Captain Lewis did not get so mad, and Captain Clark was just relieved that it was a minor injury that could be cured in 20 days (Lewis, *Journals* 362). I guess he was just as tired and anxious to get home as the rest of us.

However, some were not as anxious to get home as I was. For instance, John Colter, another private, decided to go back to the west and decided to live as a fur trapper near Yellowstone. I wanted to share the glory of the success of the expedition with all of the crew present, but some people are just meant to go their own way. After departing from Private Colter, the expedition had to say "adieu" to Sacagawea and Charbonneau as well. They decided to stay with the Mandan Indians, and the expedition paid Charbonneau $500.33 for their work (Holloway 201). Although Sacagawea did not receive anything, Clark offered to take her son to St. Louis and educate him. I always thought of Captain Clark as a hardened military officer with a calloused heart, bound to law and order, but he proved to be awfully kind-hearted. However, Charbonneau told him that his son was too young to be separated from his mother. On the way, we also stopped by the grave of Sergeant Floyd, the one who died from unknown gut pain (Chidsey, *Lewis* 154). Leaving some of our valuable members behind, we journeyed on.

Finally, on September 23rd, 1806, we reached St. Louis. Surprisingly, the whole town greeted and congratulated our successful journey, and Governor Grinder celebrated us as well. We shot our pistols in the air as an expression of our joy (Snyder 197). Persevering through the extremities of our basic needs including hunger and heat, I felt on that day the journey was worthwhile. Many of us were invited to numerous dinners (Duncan 246). We all deserved it. We carried out all of President Jefferson's instructions, traveled 8,000 miles, and brought vast information on flora, fauna, the geology, and the inhabitants of the new territory. I received 320 acres of land from the government and the double of my back pay (Holloway 214). Also, all of our names were assigned to places, mountains, or rivers we have been through.

Captain Clark tried to keep in touch with all the crew, so from him, I could hear more news about Captain Lewis and Captain Clark himself. Captain Lewis and Clark received 1,600 acres of land and plus

77

$1,128 in double pay (Snyder 198). Captain Lewis was appointed the Governor of the Missouri Territory in 1813, but Captain Lewis died two years later at the age of thirty-five. Captain Clark became the Brigadier General of Militia of Louisiana and also Superintendent of Indian Affairs (Holloway 214). Throughout the journey, I could really see the other side of Captain Clark, and he did not forget the promise with Charbonneau and Sacagawea. Captain Clark took charge of the boy and put him to St. Louis University High School in 1810.

I am not surprised now why Captain Clark was the way he was. Captain Clark was born in Caroline County, Virginia on August 1st, 1770. His five brothers fought in the Revolutionary War, but he was too young to participate. In 1789, Captain Clark joined the volunteer militia. Ever since then, Captain Clark always kept a journal even though his grammar and spelling were incorrect (Ambrose, *Lewis* 26). Captain Clark also kept contact with all the men, but all of us eventually dispersed throughout the country. Some began their career as a fur trapper, some as an author of their journals, and some very unfortunately died from natural causes accidents, unrelated to the Lewis and Clark Expedition (Duncan 248). We had spent about two years on the mission, and shed tears and sweats together. Whatever the Captains instructed us to do, we followed. I am proud of the fact that I took part in making the history of the United States. My name might not be remembered, but my determination and passion will be remembered.

Bibliography

Ambrose, Stephen E. *Lewis & Clark : Voyage of Discovery*. Washington D.C.: National Geographic Society, 1998.

- - -. *Undaunted Courage*. New York: Simon & Schuster, 1996.

Betts, Robert B. *In Search of York: The Slave Who Went to the Pacific with Lewis and Clark*. Boulder, Colorado: Colorado Associated University Press, 1985.

Chidsey, Donald B. *Lewis and Clark: The Great Adventure*. New York: Crown Publishers, Inc., 1970.

- - -. *Louisiana Purchase*. New York: Crown Publishers, Inc., 1972.

Duncan, Dayton. *The Journey of the Corps of Discovery: Lewis and Clark*. New York: Alfred A. Knopf, 1997.

Holloway, David. *Lewis and Clark and the Crossing of North America*. London: Saturday Review Press, 1974.

Jefferson, Thomas. "Instructions to Meriwether Lewis." Reproduced in History Resource Center. Farmington Hills, MI: Gale. <http://galenet.galegroup.com/servlet/HistRC/>

Lewis, Meriwether, and William Clark. "Expedition Underway: May 14-august 24,1804." *Lewis and Clark Journals* (2003).

Lewis, Meriwether. *The Expedition of Lewis and Clark*, March of America Facsimile Series, Vol. I and II. Number 56, University Microfilms, Inc., Ann Arbor, Philadelphia, 1966.

Snyder, Gerald S. *In the Footsteps of Lewis and Clark*. New York: National Geographic Society, 1970.

Staloff, Darren. *Hamilton, Adams, Jefferson : the Politics of Enlightenment and the American Founding.* New York: Hill and Wang, 2005.

White, Charles E. "Outfitting the Corps of Discovery." *Bnet.* Aug. 2003. <http://findarticles.com/p/articles/mi_qa3723/is_200308/ai_n9273 187>. (Retrieved on July 17, 2008)

"My Soccer Life"
Michael Chon (Charles DeWolf Middle School, New Jersey, USA)

Soccer is a sport I've been dedicated to for six years. My passion in soccer began in first grade at the age of six. At first, I started playing soccer in a local league. Everyday I waited until Sunday so I could go back out onto the field and kick the ball into the net. I loved the sport, so

"My Soccer Life"

I played just for the enjoyment of running and kicking. The first team I ever played for was the Fort Lee Routers in New Jersey. I was the only non-white kid in the team out of 13 people. Given that Fort Lee is known as a largely Korean area in New Jersey, this is very significant. But it is actually not surprising if you understand Korean parents and Korean families. Korean parents prefer to teach music or art to their children. I don't know any Korean parents who encourage their children to pursue little league baseball or little league soccer, except for my parents.

I guess my parents are not typical Korean parents in the USA. Most Korean kids have parents who immigrated from Korea after they graduated from college in Korea. And these first-generation Koreans in Fort Lee either own dry cleaners or work for the LG corporate office in the area. Unlike most Korean parents, my Korean parents grew up in the USA and went to college in the USA. My father is SUNY engineer-turned-entrepreneur, who started a successful telecommunications company in New Jersey. My dad, Jason Chon, is the Chairman and CEO of Locus Telecommunications, a telecommunications company with its own satellite in space, providing telecommunications services and equipment to businesses and individuals alike. My mother is fiercely intelligent as she is beautiful (that's where I get my good looks). She is a RPI graduate with a degree in biology, who is my father's right hand. They are both fluent in Korean and in English and are completely comfortable in white American as well as completely Korean social circles. Their friends are a list of Who's Who among the elite Koreans in the USA. They are quite different from Korean parents who came to the USA after graduating college in Korea, who still struggle with the English language. I guess, in many ways my dad the big shot corporate executive and a self-made millionaire prefers that his son play a man's sport like soccer than take up an easel and paint brushes. The winner in the dog-eat-dog world of business wants his first-born to shoot hoops, rather than hold a violin to his neck. (I get my competitiveness from my dad.) It's not typical of Korean parents, I tell you. But I am glad that my dad is who he is. And my mom is even more enthusiastic about my playing soccer. I guess (although I hate to admit it publicly), I have to confess that my parents are "cool" parents.

But still, when I first played soccer, I felt a bit out of place. All of the first grade Korean friends I had either started playing a musical

82

instrument, such as piano, and received specialized academic tutoring at the same time; I was the only Korean in a heavily Korean populated city of Fort Lee, New Jersey, to start a sport at a such a young age.

The reason I picked the option of joining sports rather than studying is that I loved to run and play sports. Sports have always been my passion, and enjoy the competition. If it includes running, effort, and practice for victory, I will do it. It's also teamwork that's a factor in the game, and I enjoy playing together with friends and people that I know to achieve a victory, together. I guess I have some of my dad's team leadership coupled with the desire to win in my blood.

By second grade I made the Fort Lee all-star team, and I got more serious about it. I was one of the youngest players on the team for the team was made up of second and third graders. Yet, I was a guaranteed starter and played forward for my team. We were in the best division in the league, and we finished coming in third place. I was always commented on how quick of a learner I was, and my coach told me that I had a natural talent in soccer. When I'm on the soccer field, all I think about is how to score a goal, and I try my best to complete that thought into reality.

When I was in 3rd grade I moved to a whole new town and changed schools. With a new school came a new soccer team. In the beginning of the season and coming from such a competitive league, I thought that this new club team was a joke. The team in Fort Lee was in A- division while the Northern Valley Soccer Club was in F- division. But I was determined to remain humble and become a factor in elevating the game. I was determined to become one of the players who will make the team better.

The first season was way too easy for me, but I still worked very hard to be an important part of the winning team. So, we usually won all our games by at least three goals. The Northern Valley Soccer Club finished in the top of the chart with a record of 9-1. I was thankful for Coach Matt, whom I credit with producing the winning team. He taught be to be a better soccer player; I learned new soccer techniques from him, which came in handy when scoring winner goals. Through hard work and great guidance, I dominated in all the competitions. I scored plenty of goals as a forward; I probably had the most in the league.

I guess my wish came true for the following year because we moved up two flights into the C- division. We were one of the top teams in that division as well. Now the competition between B and C divisions are fierce, so as soon as we made it up, there we were sent right back down after finishing the season 3-7. Of course, we never gave up and worked hard to get back to get to the higher division we achieved and lost. Two seasons later, we succeeded in going back to the B- division. And this time, we didn't do too poorly and ended up 4-1-5.

In 7th to 8th grade, our whole team changed. The soccer team was still in the B- division when we acquired new players like Giovanni, Stephen, James, and Palo. But Giovanni came first in 7th grade, and our whole team improved a lot that year. We were more advanced and formed great superstars on the team. We have Giovanni and Jack playing center midfield, and they both have precise passing, almost as good as David Beckam can bend a ball. Our forwards, which including me and my friend Michael, are some of the fastest people in the league. And our defense is controlled by Paul, who is the best player to have when clearing a ball in a desperate situation. The same year that Giovanni came, we moved up to the A-flight. A-Flight is definitely a tough division, and to be in it is clearly a great accomplishment. In the spring of 2008, my team and I had our first season in the A-division. Our team was up against a huge challenge that was much harder than any of us could have suspected.

One of the best games I had that season was against the Americans when I scored four goals and won the game 4-1. To come off an injury and score four goals the following game just made my day. The same season, I joined two other elite teams. The Fairview Soccer Club was a U-14 MAPS team and was one of the best in the state. MAPS is a whole different organization that holds only the most elite soccer teams. Also, another team I joined and had much success in was the select team, Ridgewood Torres. There were four major tournaments over the summer. Two of them I missed because I was in Korea, but the other two, I made. In the first tournament in which I participated, we finished in second place, but in the Regional Tournament, we came in first. It was a huge accomplishments for all us, and we were ranked 18th in the state. To be the 18th best team in the state is spectacular, and I was thrilled to be a part of making the team great. The coach of the Ridgewood team is one of the administrators of the MAPS league, and he thought I have a shot at the pros. I appreciate his encouragement, and I will strive to be a better soccer player.

This fall we had a new open tryout in Northern Valley and gained spectacular players such as Palo, Stephen, and James. Our team drastically went up to Premier Flight; we were one of the teams qualifying in the highest division! Finally, we became one the top teams in the entire soccer organization.

Last year, in 7th grade, I made the school soccer team. We had 20 kids on the team from grade 6th to 8th grade. Our team was one of the best teams and came in 2nd place with a record of 13-1-2. It's a very impressive record. What's even more impressive is that we won a hard fought championship. It was between Old Tappan and Haworth at the high school turf. We won 2-0 in which two substitutes scored. Our whole school came to watch in the snowing weather and it was a fun, tough game. Everybody was hyper and jumpy the whole game.

This year, my 8th grade year, was even better. The Northern Valley Championship was held on November 5th, 2008, at Northern Valley Regional High School, Demarest. My team played against Demarest Middle School for the championship title on their turf. My father and mother were there supporting me and encouraging me as they do for my every soccer game (except when my dad is away on a business trip). You can imagine the tension between two neighboring towns. Our team was at a disadvantage because we were playing in the grounds of our enemy team. But we held our determination, and I was completely focused on winning. I wanted to play with my team to bring my friends, who are my team members, to victory. I wanted to share sweet joy of victory with them. So, I tried my best. I tried to find extra energy to win this championship for the team, for myself, and for my parents. The game was tense. But when the championship was all over, we won by score of 3-2. I scored the winning goal!

My soccer life so far has been as great as it could possibly be. I've had plenty of accomplishments and look forward to a great future of soccer victories. Whichever team I play for will have my complete devotion and winning spirit. I will work with my team to bring home the trophies and make my soccer team shine. Whichever school I play for, I am determined to grow together with the team and lead it to victory for the pride of the whole school. I have done that so far. There is a reason why I am the President of Charles DeWolf Middle School. Students at DeWolf Middle School know that they could count on me to lead them to victory not only in sports but in all of our program. And with the winning spirit that my dad has given me in my genes, I will apply myself to bringing victory wherever I go and to whatever organization I belong to. I am determined to win and to benefit my team.

SORA YANG

"Koreans in Sydney, Australia"
Sora Yang (Baulkham Hills Selective High School, AUSTRALIA)

Where am I?
I'm in the smallest continent, the 6th largest country in the world.
I'm in a land of extremes and diversity.
I'm where there's the largest natural harbour in the world[1],
I'm where there's a beautiful house –

---

[1] http://www,wikipedia.org/Sydney/

White, but not the White House –
This is a house made of *'shells'*.

On the world map:
33° 52' S, 151° 12'E.[2]
A place called –
Sydney.

A place that's both very new and old. A place that reflects the amalgamation of the 40,000 years of history of the Aborigines[3] (the native people of Australia), and the recent 200 years' history of the first English settlers.

And of course, the even younger history of the migrants.

I am one of us Koreans living in Sydney, Australia.

A History and Observation of Koreans and Korean Culture in Australia:

Part 1: The First Arrivals.

Koreans have been coming to Australia since the 1920's[4], in minute numbers, but it was only in 1957 that the first ever Korean person received citizenship[5] (identity unknown), recorded in the 1958 Australian Yearbook. This was in the aftermath of the Korean War; it is likely the unnamed, newly naturalized citizen was either the Korean wife of an Australian solider, or one of the Korean orphans of the war, adopted by Australians.

---

[2] Ibid.
[3] Ibid.
[4] 호주한인 50 년사 편찬위원회, **호주한인 50 년사** (서울: 진흥, 2008), p.3
[5] Ibid. p.607

Part 1 a): Significant Early Arrivals.

A significant literary figure and one of the first Asian-Australian published authors[6], Don O' Kim (Kim Don Ho) was one of the early immigrants to Australia; in 2003, he received the Australian Writer's Emeritus Award.[7]
Another noteworthy figure is that of Woo Jaerin, who became the first chairman of the Korean Society of Sydney in 1968[8].

However, the first invited immigrant to Australia was Choi Yong Gil[9], who came to Australia with his wife and 15 month-old daughter in 1968. As a youth, he had worked as an interpreter with Australian soldiers in the Korean War – after the war, it is thought he kept up a correspondence with the Australian soldiers he had worked with, who paved the way for an invitation of permanent residency by the Australian government to Choi Yong Gil.

Part 2: Further Arrivals.

After the initial invitation received by Choi Yong Gil, there was an increased flow of immigrants invited to Australia, namely, skilled migrants. Due to the substandard quality of life of Korea in the years following the Korean War, those that could make a living in other countries left Korea. It was these migrants that came to Australia – specialists and skilled workers. Among them, there were Korean nurses who had been working in West Germany, who immigrated to Australia (1968~79)[10], as well as Taekwondo masters (1964~65)[11] and geographers

---

[6] http://www.asianaustralianstudies.org/resources.html#do
[7] 호주한인 50 년사 편찬위원회, *호주한인 50 년사*(서울: 진흥, 2008), p.652
[8] Ibid. p.32
[9] Ibid. p.40
[10] Ibid. p.65
[11] Ibid. p.45

"KOREANS IN SYDNEY, AUSTRALIA"

$(1971)^{12}$ from Korea. Even so, the numbers of these immigrants were minor, especially compared to the numbers of skilled migrants today.

The trend of immigration to Australia continued, in 1976, Korean soldiers who had fought in the Vietnam War came to Australia, initially on tourist visas which they had overstayed – but the Australian government granted mass permanent residency visas to the 486 people.[13] This amnesty was later on repeated two more times, to skilled migrants only.

In the 1980's, different immigration policies were established, one of these being the 'Regularisation of Status Program', which meant immigration was viable through family connections. This led to a massive increase in immigration numbers, an increase of 500 people a year changing their visa status to permanent residency.[14]

Another policy was that concerning business and skilled migration (1986), which led to a further increase of skilled, and wealthy migrants, many of whom started businesses and lived a more comfortable lifestyle than those of the earlier migrants.[15]

Yet, another policy which has accepted Koreans into Australia is that which relates to overseas students in Australia, making it possible for students to come to Australia to study. Although this policy was established in the 80's, it was only in 1993, after the Korean government removed barriers to international travel that there was a substantial increase in overseas students coming to Australia.[16]

The final policy to date is the working holiday visa (1995) which allows people to come in to Australia to both work and holiday in Australia. Like the overseas student policy, it was some time before this policy had much effect, it was only in the 2000's, after the publicity derived from

---

[12] Ibid. p.46
[13] Ibid. p.62
[14] Ibid. p.75
[15] Ibid p.656
[16] Ibid. p.244

the Sydney Olympics that there was an explosive increase in the number of Koreans entering Australia on the working holiday visa.[17]

In recent years, there has been an increasing trend of high school, and even primary school, students coming to Australia to study English. Korean parents in Korea are obsessive about their children's education, especially their child's English skills - the practice of a parent remaining in Korea (to earn money), while their spouse lives overseas with their child, for their child's English education is increasingly widespread – hence the term 'girohgi' (기러기) parents.

Part 3: Demographics:

1. The Settlement of Koreans in Australia.

Did you know?

24% of Australian residents were born outside of Australia. That's 4,956,863 people.[18]

Did you know?

In Australia, there are about 100,000 Korean people, and 63% of them live in NSW.[19]

Did you know?

In Sydney, there are 32,125 Korea-born people[20] - as a proportion of the Sydney population of 4 million, that's about 0.8%.

---

[17] Ibid. p.94-95
[18] http://en.wikipedia.org/wiki/Immigration_to_Australia
[19] Ibid.
[20] http://www,wikipedia.org/Sydney/

It seems an insignificant number, doesn't it? But we 32,125 have a substantial presence, scattered in key areas, as can be seen circled in the map below.

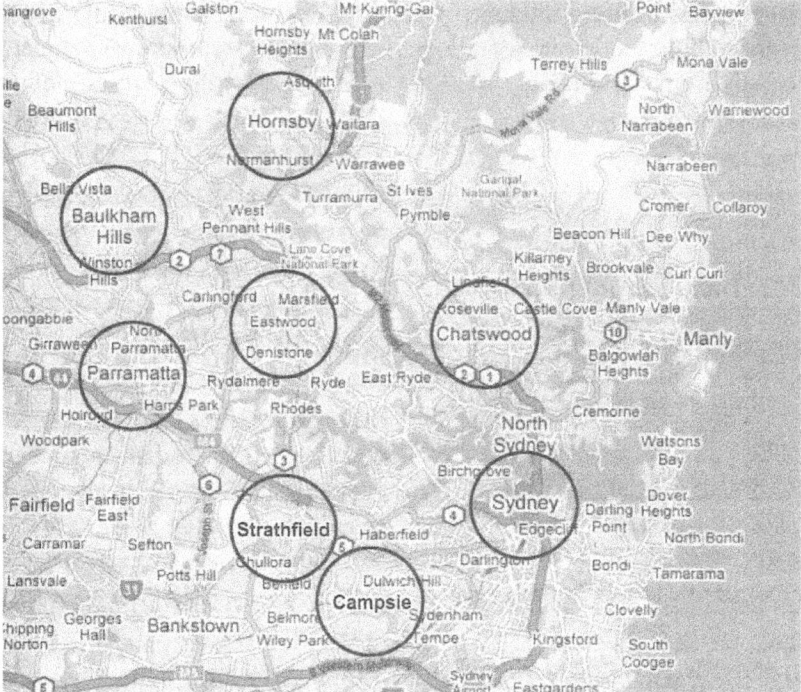

Map. 호주한인 50 년사 편찬위원회, **호주한인 50 년사**(서울: 진흥, 2008, p.173)

Campsie, of the Canterbury area was the first 'Korea Town'. The early immigrants and their families tended to settle here, and until 2001, it was the center of Korean settlement.[21] However, it has since been receding in importance, its growth in terms of population and activity of Koreans outpaced by newer suburbs.

---

[21] 호주한인 50 년사 편찬위원회, **호주한인 50 년사**(서울: 진흥, 2008), p.176

Chatswood is another area with a strong Korean presence - company employees and their families tend to congregate here, because of it's proximity to the city's CBD area.

Strathfield, like Chatswood, is close to the city, and the Korean population is made up of a majority of short term Korean students, in Australia to learn English – many of them attending language schools for Korean students based in the city.

Epping, Eastwood and Hornsby, of the Hornsby Area have been the emerging suburbs in terms of growth and importance. It has been mainly the skilled and business Koreans of the later immigrant arrivals that have settled here.

(I live in the unspecified suburb of Beecroft, a predominantly Caucasian suburb, between Eastwood and Hornsby, near the West Pennant Hills area.)

2. Jobs and Businesses.

The areas of concentration in terms of jobs and businesses are, predictably, identical to those of demographics. However, in terms of jobs, the areas of types of jobs vary widely – from blue collar all the way to white collar workers. Presently, Korean people working in blue collar jobs tend to work in plumbing, mechanics, cleaning, painting, factory workers, restaurant workers, tiling etc. Initial immigrants tend to work in low-skilled jobs, that don't require high English skills. However, at the other end of the scale, there are many white collar workers: accountants, computer programmers, and lawyers, among others.

In recent years, Koreans are entering the political scene on a local level – due to the significant Korean population in Strathfield; as of this September 2008, the first ever Korean Mayor has been elected to the Strathfield Council.

In terms of businesses, there is, quite literally, anything you need. In Eastwood in particular there are Korean DVD/video stores, grocery stores, clothing stores, health product stores, book stores, manhwa stores, stationary & accessory stores.

Services include restaurants and cafes, optometrists, hair salons, doctors, Chinese medicine practitioners, lawyers, immigration consultants, travel agents, accountants, service trade people, newspapers and magazines.
Korean culture: There's the Baduk Club, Taekwondo training centers, churches, hakwon (coaching/tutoring centers), information center for overseas students, norasebang (Korean karaoke), and Korean movies aired at the Reading Cinemas in the city.

While this is a list of services that are Korean, and managed by Koreans, it's important to realize that Koreans in Australia aren't limited to living exclusively within the Korean community – many, many Koreans have jobs in non-Korean firms.

We've been incorporated into the Australian culture – we retain our cultural identity while still being part of a whole that is Australia.

Part 4: Culture: Churches and Korean Culture in the Wider Community.

Churches and Korean Language Schools are vital organisations in maintaining Korean culture and language in the general Korean society. The first Korean church was established in Melbourne, in 1973, and it was in the following year that the first Korean church was established in Sydney[22].

Presently (2005), there are 200 churches in Australia, and 130 of them are in Sydney, as well as two Catholic Churches and one Buddhist temple[23].

Churches play a critical role in bringing together people of the Korean community; it's a place where people young and old can meet celebrate

---

[22] Ibid. p.144
[23] Ibid. p.151

their ethnicity together – many of the larger churches also run Korean Language classes.

The first Korean Language School was established in Redfern, in 1973. Presently, there are 40 Korean Language Schools[24], usually held on Saturdays.

However, it is not only in Korean Language Schools that the Korean language is practiced, Korean is also an optional HSC subject, 12 primary schools have Korean as a mandatory second language class, and there are Korean Studies departments at various universities.[25]

There are also various programs to encourage Korean skills and knowledge of culture – one of which being the Korean Reading Book Club, designed with the aim of encouraging the reading of Korean books and discussing Korean literature and its forms, administered by the Korean consulate - various scholarships and exchange programs to Korea are also available.

However, it's not always been smooth sailing for Korean culture to have a firm foothold in Australia. Back in 2004, The Department of Education proposed to get rid of Korean Education Advisor – however, there was a public outcry and protest, and in the end, the Korean Government stated it would donate sums towards the continuation of the program. An agreement was reached, the "Memorandum of Understanding'[26], which detailed the continuing legacy of Korean language and culture to be retained in Australia.

Part 5: My Perspective.

From here on in, this will be a personal view, my view, of Koreans in Sydney, Australia:

---

[24] Ibid. p.234
[25] Ibid. p.246
[26] Ibid. p. 244

Number-wise, we aren't a very intimidating force, but our influence spreads far beyond mere numbers – in the wake of the Korean Wave, various aspects of Korean culture are well known in the Asian community. In my experience, Korean entertainment (music, bands, and dramas), food, and even our language are popular, especially in the general Asian student community. My Chinese friends know more about Korean dramas than I do, and are more fanatical about Korean bands than I am.

Although this may be because of my context of being surrounded by Asian students at school, no one can doubt the preponderance of the Korean culture in certain areas – particularly, in my personal experience, Eastwood and Strathfield, and to a lesser extent, Epping. While I actually haven't been to the 'Korea Town' of Strathfield very often, I do know for a fact that Strathfield is a veritable "Korea Town" – from what I've seen, around the plaza area near the train station; wherever you turn, at least every two out of three stores have big signs in Korean, as well as English, and it's nearly impossible not to run into a Korean person. However, in recent times, Eastwood is becoming increasingly 'Korean' – it's divided into two distinct halves – the "Korean" side, and the "Chinese" side, a concept that has become fact, at least among the student population. My favourite hairdressing salon is there, as well as my dentist, my optometrist, and my G.P.

Epping, too, is becoming more 'Korean' – there are the usual Korean restaurants, hairdressers and grocery stores.

As you can see, areas with strong Korean population concentrations are literal 'Korea Towns', they're pieces of Korea in a smaller and more relaxed scale.

So what do my friends and I do when we go out for outings? Usually, on whole-day outings in the holidays, we go to the city to do the usual, ordinary, sixteen-year-old-girl things– go shopping, sometimes we watch a movie, take photos, eat at restaurants. Most days, we go to a noraebang (Korean karaoke) and (attempt) to sing for a few hours - even my non-Korean friends can sing along to parts of popular Korean songs.

I've been incredibly blessed, to be able to grow up the way I have, to have had the experiences I've lived, to know the people I've met. My parents were part of 1993 influx of overseas students, and it was at the airport we met our first Korean acquaintances, and one of my almost closest, almost literally since-birth-friend, Namhee Koo. We're still in touch, despite having gone to different high schools.

"KOREANS IN SYDNEY, AUSTRALIA"

We're not alone in Australia, my uncle and his family have come out to Australia since – he's one of the 'skilled migrants', a computer technician.

So here we are.

In retrospect, the writing of this essay has caused to me to realize the depth and history of Korean settlement in Australia, to think beyond what it is now, and realize what has been.

As Koreans in Sydney, of Australia:

Here we've been, we are, and will be.

"Incredible Memories from Korea"
Andy Jung (Charles DeWolf Middle School, New Jersey, USA)

Korea is a really small country compared to other countries. Korea is about 99,800 km². During Holiday, highways are always traffic-jammed, and it takes forever to get to somewhere. But in the United States of America, the traffic is often better flowing compared to Korea. There are about 49 million people in Korea.

My name is Andy Jung. I was born in Seoul, Korea, on November 26ᵗʰ, 1996, in hospital named Samsung Jaeil Hospital. My dad's name is Min Yong Jung and my mother's name is OkYun Lee. I lived in an apartment at 7ᵗʰ floor with my family. When I was 5 years old, I moved to another area called Do Bong Ku. Do Bong Ku is located in Seoul, Korea. I lived in 3ʳᵈ floor in apartment. An apartment that I lived in was really great. There were mountains around, so lots of bugs like dragonflies, and others. The air was fresh and clean.

When I was in Korea, I used to hang out with my friends. We did lots of things like Yu-Gi-Oh cards. It's kind of card game. I played with lots of items. Sometimes I travel around my town. I went to anywhere like somebody's house and big markets to play games. I started traveling around my town when I was about 4th grade with my friends. My friends whom I traveled with were 'Jay Man Yu', 'Jay Suk Yu' and others. It was adventurous, so I liked it.

In Korea, we had to go to lots of institutes, like for English, instruments, math, and others. I did English, math, and instrument. I started playing piano when I was 5 years old, and now I am still playing. I started piano and did not stop because I liked music. Music made me feel happy. I started from beginning like Do, Le, Mi, Pa, Sol La, Si. I wasn't really good in the beginning. After I mastered that, I started playing songs by using those codes (Do, Le, Mi Pa, Sol, La, Si). I kept and kept playing, and now I'm playing Cherini 30. It's a pretty high level. Sometimes, I play jazz music. My favorite jazz was Canon. I memorized it. My teacher is now the same teacher as my friend Jake's. Jake is better than me, but still, I will practice and become better than Jake.

Next, I did math at an institute (hakwon). In Korea, math is really important. Korean teachers are really severe. When I did something wrong, the math teacher hit me with a stick. But I tried to remain positive. When I have a break during math class, I always went to supermarket with my friends. I bought foods and other things to eat in class. For example, I bought chips, drinks, or gum. My teacher let us eat food in class, but my teacher told us not to chew gum, but I chewed gum anyway. I never got into trouble for chewing gum, though. Sometimes, it took me 10 minutes to choose what to buy at the supermarket to eat. If I was late for class, teacher would scream at us. When class was about to finish in 5 minutes, teacher gave us homework. Good thing was that she gave little amount of homework. People hate institutes.

In Korea, I went to elementary school named Nuwon Elementary School. We walked to school, not like in America. In America, my parents pick me up. My apartment was really close to my school in Korea, but sometimes, I was late for school because I woke up late. In Korea, school ends at 1:30 P.M. or 12:00 P.M. Korean schools were pretty fun because we didn't take tests seriously, unlike in America. I studied really a lot when I have a test in U.S., but in Korea, I didn't really have to. I had the same teacher for all the subject, except English. I had English, art, math, science, Korean, social studies, music, and Physical Education. We had a lot more science experiments than in U.S. schools. We did lots of fun and different experiments. For example, like making soda, cotton candy, and others. Everything was not that hard but not too easy. It was fine for me.

My favorite part of school was going to "sherp" when I was 4th grade. It took 2 hours from school to the camp place, or sherp place. We separated into 2 groups for boys and girls. And of course, we slept separately, like boys with boys and girls with girls. We slept in a wooden house. I was the captain, or the leader, of the boys. During sherp, we learned many things, like how to talk with your hand, about mysteries, and others. We couldn't sleep late. If we played at night, the instructor would force us to do 50 push-ups or run around 3 miles. We had to wake up at 7:30 A.M. to 8:30 A.M. We stretched and started learning or we hiked on a mountain. Last day of sherp, we bought items in the gift shop. At night, we did CAMPFIRE! It was the best! We danced and sang. We sang jazz songs, but I do not remember the songs. It was great, but the stupid part was that instructors told us some kind of story about how our parents are really important. They told us how parents take care of us, and how much they love us. More stupid thing was that almost everyone cried! Of course, I did not cry. Next day, we all went back home. One of my favorite parts of the sherp was when someone pooped and the toilet couldn't flush. Smell was really bad, so my friends kept on spraying with orange flavor spray. It was really disgusting, and funny.

My other favorite part of my school was parties. I had Ramen Party at school. I had ramen party about 2 or 3 time in a month. There were about 24 people in a party and a teacher. A ramen is a noodle with hot spicy soup. We brought our own cup ramen. My teacher brought hot water for ramen, and he gave us hot water, one by one, into our cup ramen and we ate it. People brought big, normal or small size cup ramen, and they brought different types of cup ramen. For example, they brought not spicy, little spicy, really spicy, or with seafood.

While we are eating cup ramen, we watched movies. We watched 'Shin Chan Movie', 'Pokemon Movie', and 'Harry Potter and Goblet of Fire'. Shin Chan Movie was about a main character named Shin Chan, 7 year old boy saving the world. Pokemon is a type of a

101

monster to fight with other people. Pokemon Movie is about a main character named Ash saving 2 legendary pokemon named Latios, and Latias. They get kidnapped by 2 evil women, and Ash is trying to save them. Harry Potter and Goblet of Fire is, as we all know, about a main character named Harry Potter. By accident, he went to the magic tournament and tried to win. It was really fun.

Other party was making our own food. It was at the same place as for Ramen Party. For example, I made hamburger with my friends. Others made other foods like cake, sushi and others. We brought our own materials, and we made any food we wanted to. School parties were great. There were same amount of people as Ramen party and the same teacher.

My 4th grade homeroom teacher was a man named 'Don Su Jun'. He has long hair, and wears glasses. He is younger than my mother. He is married and has a son. He liked to take a photo of our class. He took lots of photos during every field trip, and he showed the photos to us the day after the field trip. He went to Seoul National University (SNU). Seoul Natinal University is the best university in Korea, but the Ivy League is better than Seoul National University. He is a really good, kind and smart teacher. He is the BEST teacher ever.

There are many holidays in Korea. For example, Sulnal, Taeborum, Hansiknal, Dano, Chusok, Constitution Day, Liberation Day, National Foundation Day and others. Sulnal is the greatest holiday in Korea. We get up early on that day and wear new clothes to observe a memorial service to the ancestors. At that day, my relatives come to my house and celebrate together. That day, I play with my cousins. I play computer games, play outside or watch TV.

The 15th day of January is Taeborum. We eat chestnuts, peanuts, and walnuts to get free boils or furuncles on that day. In the evening, families go out and enjoy seeing the full moon and pray to it for good luck.

In March, there is a holiday called Hansiknal. On this day, people go to their ancestor's tombs and make them clean and neat, planting young trees around them. That day, there is lots of traffic jams.

The Dano Festival falls on the 5th of May by the lunar calendar. This is one of the oldest holidays in Korea, and it is still observed by a few people. On this day, both men and women wash their hair with the water boiled with iris herbs, wishing for good luck. Also, young boys play Ssirum that day. Ssirum is Korea wrestling. I never played Ssirum because I lived in a city, so my town had no place for Ssirum.

Chusok is one of the greatest holidays in Korea. It's like Korean Thanksgiving Day. Chusok comes on August 15th by the lunar calendar. Nearly all the people return to their homes to celebrate the holiday. We prepare rice cakes, wines and various dishes made with the newly harvested crops and go to our ancestor's graves. I went to a grave once before I came to U.S.A. I went to my grandpa's grave. We eat Songpyon on this day. Songpyon is a rice cake containing sweet beans or sesame in it. I ate them for more than 5 years. It's sweet and good.

July 17 is Constitution Day. The day is one of the most significant national holidays. On that day in 1948, the Constituent National Assembly promulgated the Constitution of the Republic based on democracy.

"Incredible Memories from Korea"

The 15th of August is Liberation Day, the anniversary of the liberation in 1945 from the Japanese occupation of Korea (1910-1945). Various events, including a military parade, take place on this day.

The 3rd of October is National Foundation Day. The government holds a ceremony for the nation's birthday.

I like holidays because on holidays, I get to skip school. Just like U.S.A, we get to skip school and celebrate the holiday with our family and get to play with cousins. I think it's the best.

There are lots of important places in Korea. For example, like in U.S.A., important places are like Empire State building. In Korea there are important places like Kyongbok Palace. Kyongbok Palace is a palace, and it was completed by King T'aejo. It was named Kyongbok Palace which means "a shining palace."

Another important place is The National Folk Museum. It is located within Kyongbok Palace. The museum is a wonderful place, celebrating thousands of years of Korean culture. Over four thousand items are on display, and they are designed to be educational.

These important places are really educational. I went to lots important places like Kyongbok Palace, the National Folk Museum, and others. It really helped me.

Korea is way better than United States of America. There are more cool holidays, cool parties in school, and other things. Even though Korea is weak, and a small country, I still love my home.

"Why I Like to Cook with My Mom"
Gloria Bae (Tenakill Middle School, New Jersey, USA)

I enjoy cooking with my mom because she makes it fun, and I like the fact that cooking can almost always be a hands-on experience. When your mom is making cooking fun and you like how it's a hands-on experience, you won't be able to not like cooking. I enjoy it a lot. Now, I'll specifically describe exactly why I like to cook with my mom.

Like I said before, one of the reasons why I like to cook with my mom is that she makes it fun. Exactly how, you may ask? Well, she makes it fun by singing songs, dancing, and also by telling hilarious jokes. My mom sings all different kinds of songs. She sings opera, classic, pop, praises, and so much more. Usually, when my mom starts to sing, I know the song as well and start to sing along. My mom also dances while she cooks, too. Once, she and I were square dancing while waiting for a couple of ingredients to cook. It was a very interesting experience for me to square dance with my mom because I didn't know that my mother could dance! Not just square dancing, I thought she didn't know how to dance at all! This experience with my mom makes me feel really happy and proud of her because you pretty well know that most moms either can't or don't dance with their daughters while in the middle of cooking food. Lastly, not only does my mom sing and dance, she tells really funny jokes too! Sometimes, she tells some of the jokes that she heard, but sometimes, she makes up her own jokes and they turn out to be as equally funny as the jokes that she's heard. She usually sings, dances, and tells really funny jokes while we wait for food to cook or boil, or before or after we cook. I love the way that she is able to make a first cooking experience really fun.

Also, the second reason why I like to cook is that I like the fact that cooking is a hands-on experience. When I am cooking with my mom, I usually do the washing, cutting, chopping, and don't forget the last part...tasting! My mom doesn't often let me use the stove because after I got burned once, she didn't really let me near the stove again. But, my mom has me taste the food; I have a really strong sense of taste. I can taste almost anything in a food, even if it's hidden, while others can't find it. The tasting part is my favorite.

Besides cooking, my favorite hands-on thing to do is arts and crafts. I like arts and crafts, and my favorite hands-on activity is making pop-ups. Pop-ups are shapes and figures made of different materials that make it look like it's popping up at you, or in other words, that make it look like it's 3-D. They are very interesting and no matter what age you are, you'll like them. In fact, my grandfather and my cousin, Sophia, also like to make pop-ups.

Sophia is my favorite cousin. She is currently five years old and is having the best time of her life in kindergarten. Just wait until she gets older like me. She'll take the world by a storm. Right now, the only things she likes about school are that she gets to meet new people and that she gets to learn to read and write. Even though she is only a little child, she is very interested in academics. Since she is only five, she enjoys playing what other little girls play. She likes to play with her Barbies and she also likes to play dress up. When I say "dress up", I don't mean that she dresses herself up. She always has someone to dress up. And that someone is always me. Some people may think that this is funny, but it is actually not because thanks to my favorite cousin, I now have to be able to fit into her clothes, and that is almost impossible for me to do. But, even though I want to protest and tell her that I'm too old to play dress up with her, I can't because she has cute little puppy eyes that are each at least the size of a considerably large orange.

Some people take one look at us and blurt out the same question over and over again. The question is, "How are you two related?" When people ask us this question, Sophia and I both get really annoyed because we've had to answer this question together many times before. I always answer and the answer is always, "Can't you tell? My dad is Sophia's dad's older brother. La duh!"

The people go, "How would I know?"

"Can't you tell right away?"

"Uh... no."

"Oh, well then, that's your problem."

"Thank you?"

"No problem!"

I enjoy making things with my grandfather, who is my father's father. My grandfather is the funniest man alive, in my opinion. My extremely funny grandfather is eighty-two years old, and he is strong and healthy. He loves Jesus with all of his heart, which is a good thing. My grandfather is currently abiding in Flushing, New York, with his wife, who is my grandmother. What I like most about him is that he can make anybody laugh at any time. For example, once, when I was extremely sick, he came over to our house all the way from Flushing, just to see me. When he came over, he prayed for me, then sat around for hours reading the Bible to me and told funny jokes that made me crack up like crazy and that helped me get cured of my sickness by the morning of the next day. But, even though I know it's the praying that cured me, I'm really thankful to have such a loving eighty-two year old grandfather who drove for at least an hour just to see me. Whenever I think about this, it makes me so happy to have this amazing person related to me, and it makes me proud to be his granddaughter. Besides the fact that everyone thinks he is hilarious, I really like the fact that my grandfather has the mind of a young adult in middle school. He used to enjoy everything that I enjoy now. He used to like to hike, ride bikes, and go for long car rides.

Out of all the things that I have done with my grandfather in the past, one specific thing really stands out above all the others. This is when my grandfather and I were building the most exciting thing that anyone could possible build. We were building a model of a house. It wasn't just an ordinary house, either. It was a model of the houses from a long time ago in ancient Korea. It is made of little pieces of wood and plastic. When my grandfather and I were making this model, he told me some of the history about ancient Korea. They were all very interesting. I enjoyed being able to make cool things with him. Making the Korean model with my grandfather will be something that I will always remember until the end. I hope that my grandfather and I have the chance to make a few more things before he goes to God's kingdom where God is waiting. I will really, really, really miss my grandfather when he goes to Heaven.

I had a lot of fun with him and the thing that really stands out in my mind out of all the things that I did with him is when we were making a pop-up family photo. My grandfather and I worked hard for a few days to accomplish making this beautiful creation. First, we took the best family photo that we could find; it had to include everyone in the family, of course, and we cut it out into a rectangle. Then, my grandfather and I started on the base for the pop-up that would actually make the photo seem like it was popping out at you. We constructed the base out of cylinders that were made out of strong construction paper. We then taped them behind the photo. After all of this was done, we had the final step of framing our masterpiece. We had to be very careful about placing the artwork in the right place so that we didn't crumple it. Finally, when we finished hanging up the frame and took a look at it, we both almost fainted. Why? Well, that's because when we saw this, we were surprised at how amazingly it had turned out. I will never forget this time that helped me get closer to my grandfather than ever before, and I will always cherish this project forever.

I think that pop-ups are interesting to make because first, you have to cut all the pieces out, and then you get to tape and glue the pieces together. For example, I once made a pop-up of a dancing cat. How I made it was fairly easy, but I had to be careful, so that I wouldn't cut the wrong lines because if I did, then my pop-up would be ruined. I made this pop-up at Sophia's house, and I helped her make it. It turned out amazing and now, all she does are make pop-ups. So, you can say that appreciating pop-ups runs in the family.

I think that cooking is a hands-on activity, like making pop-ups, because when you cook, not only do you cut and chop, you also have to boil, steam, cook, fry, etc. Cooking is also a hands-on activity because instead of just microwave cooking, you physically move and use your hands.

Even though I don't quite remember when I made this dish, my favorite dish that I made with my mom is probably 잡채 (Jab-chae). I happen to remember this dish the best because while my mom and I were making this dish, we had a lot of fun. This dish is mainly made up of clear noodles, soy sauce, and basically just any type of vegetable you want in it. The toppings my family puts in are fried eggs, carrots, mushrooms, onions and spring onions. It tastes delicious when seasoned with soy sauce and topped off with sesame seeds.

First, my mom and I put the clear noodles in a pot with boiling water to cook. Then, we chopped up the carrots, onions, mushrooms, and spring onions and started to fry them on a frying pan. While my mom and I were doing these things, we were singing "Inside Out" by Hillsong. After we had set all of this up and had started cooking, my mom suddenly took my hand, pulled me away from the stove, and started to swing me in circles. We laughed and amazingly started to sing "Above All" by Hillsong at the same exact time, simultaneously and unplanned. It was a bit scary when that happened. By the time we finished singing "Above All", the food was ready.

My mom took out a big, pink bowl and dumped the clear noodles that were done cooking, and the carrots, onions, mushrooms, and spring onions that were done frying, into the bowl. Then, we seasoned it with soy sauce. Of course, I was the one to taste it first, and we topped the finally finished traditional Korean food off with sesame seeds. We each tried some and... almost fainted. It was so delicious. We asked my dad what he thought about it, and he said that he loved it. That was what we had for dinner.

When my dad, mom, and I eat dinner, we usually talk about a couple of things. We go around the dinner table and each say the most interesting thing that happened to us that day. Then, we go on and describe the whole story. My dad usually talks about what he did at the his dry cleaner's while waiting for customers. My mom and I had fun finding out that he had a picture of us as his wallpaper on his laptop. We also found out that my dad likes to read books that were written by the senior pastor in our church, Emmaus Korean Presbyterian Church in Closter, New Jersey. My mom usually either sleeps or just read the same books as my dad. The only reason my mom sleeps while I'm at school is that she usually gets up at five o' clock in the morning after going to bed at around three o' clock. My parents find out that while I'm at school, I really worked hard to get the grades that I deserve. When my parents heard this, they were really proud to have me as their daughter. I was proud to be theirs, too. These are just the things that my family talks about at the dinner table daily. Sometimes, my parents and I talk about our favorite subject: My future. My parents always say that they know I'll have no problem whatsoever to go to Harvard. They have faith in me, and they believe that I will try my best. I am sometimes stressed because of schoolwork and such, but I really have to thank God for giving me such supportive parents who are always there for me no matter what.

While we were making 잡체, I had the privilege of being able to cut and chop all of the vegetables, put the clear noodles into the pot with boiling water, and most importantly, I had the privilege of tasting the

AMAZING food that God had provided us with. Even though some people might think that this is nothing, they're wrong because I'm really proud to at least have a chance to cook with my mom.

I like to cook for the two reasons that were stated earlier. I like to cook because my mom makes it fun and because I like the fact that cooking is a hands-on experience for anybody, no matter how old they are. I love cooking. It's like my passion.

When I get a little bit older, I hope to be taught to make a few more things. I want to be taught how to make a few items for each of the three meals that we eat everyday. For breakfast meals, I want to be taught how to make waffles. That is the only thing I don't know how to make that is a part of the breakfast menu. I already know how to make scrambled eggs, pancakes, fried toasts, and bagels.

For the lunch menu, I would like to learn how to make BiBimBap. BiBimBap is one of my all-time favorite foods. It consists of rice that is mixed with all kinds of toppings, such as fried eggs, carrots, cucumbers, and maybe even a bit of beef. Most Korean people like their BiBimBap spicy, so they add a spoonful of a very spicy paste called GoChuJang. GoChuJang is made of red hot peppers, so it is extremely spicy. It tastes really good. You are supposed to eat BiBimBap with a spoon so that everything doesn't get all over your fingers. I want to learn how to make BiBimBap because this dish is one of my all-time favorites. It is absolutely delicious. Also, I would like to be taught how to make Kimchi BokeumBap. This mouthwatering dish is made up of a couple of things. It is made up of rice, Kimchi, and fried eggs. It is cooked on the frying pan and tastes absolutely delicious when steaming hot. It has a pinch of spiciness to it, which makes me like this dish even more. This, too, is also one of my favorites.

For the dinner menu, I would really like to learn how to make Kimchi Jjigae and steak. Kimchi Jjigae is also an all time favorite of mine. It is made up of vegetables, of course, kimchi, and sometimes tuna fish or bits of beef. This dish is very spicy, so no one should gulp this delicious food down. They should savor every last bit of it because it'll be just about the most delicious dish that they have ever tasted. Last, but not least, I would like to learn how to make a strawberry shortcake and a Hershey chocolate pie for dessert. Even though some of the foods may not be Korean foods, I would really like to learn them all because they really appeal to me personally.

111

"Why I Like to Cook with My Mom"

Here is a list of my all time favorite foods: They are my mom's Kimchi Jjigae, my mom's Kimchi BokeumBap, and basically just about every other food that contains kimchi. My parents' favorite foods are not as childish as mine. My mom likes Woodong, which are thick noodles that are eaten while being dipped in a hot broth, lasagna, spicy tuna rolls, red bean porridge, and Chobap. Chobap is rice that is mixed with carrots sheathed in with a big piece of egg. Some of my dad's favorite foods are chicken, LA Kalbi, and AguJjim. LA Kalbi is any kid's favorite because it is hot, juicy beef that is smothered in sweet sauce that makes your mouth water just looking at it. AguJjim is a bit of a strange dish. It consists of fish and vegetables in a hot spicy sauce. These dishes are all mouthwatering. Okay, maybe they are a bit childish, but, they are still not as childish as my favorite foods.

When I am cooking with my mom, the view of the kitchen from my point of view is amazing. It's amazing because when I look around me, there are all of the ingredients we need to cook the food with all over the kitchen, everywhere. Even though it can get a bit messy at times, we end up having the kitchen sparkling and dazzling as soon as we finish cooking dinner. Even when I grow up to be a REALLY famous law professor at Harvard, I hope to also be an amazing cook at the same time. When I grow up and become rich and famous, I want to buy an estate, instead of a house, that is really big. I want to buy a big estate, so that my family can have our own home and my parents can have their own house in the same estate. That would be really cool. Also, in my family's house, I would really like a big kitchen so that my mom and I can continue to cook together since we'll be living right next to each other. Since cooking is very important to me, I would like my kitchen to be about the size of my current basement, except, I want my kitchen to be taller. No matter what, I know that I'll always enjoy cooking with my mom. Not, only will I always enjoy cooking with my mom, I'll always love my mom until the end.

HAEBIN YOON

"When People Think of a Missionary's Kid"
Haebin Yoon (Dekar Academy, SENEGAL, AFRICA)

When people think of a missionary's kid (MK), usually they would say that they can adjust to a place easily. This is somewhat true, although it really depends on personality, the country you are going to, and the age when you arrived there. As for me, these three things made it easier for me when I came to Sierra Leone for the first time.

I was only four years old when I arrived in Sierra Leone, so it wasn't hard at all for me to adjust. I can still remember the times when I played with the neighborhood kids, who were Sierra Leonean. I had no feelings against them. I was really playful and wanted to make friends with anyone, just like now, so I had fun with my playmates until war broke out, a year after this time. Sierra Leone was engulfed in violence, bloodshed, and death.

We evacuated to Korea for a short period of time. "A short period of time" changed my view of my African friends. In Korea, I was used to see skins whiter than my African friends, so that when I came back I found myself trying to get away from them. Right now, I feel very stupid about this; but then, I was just a child who wanted things that are clean or white (I thought then that dark skin was caused by dirtiness).

That was just the start of adjusting to my environment. Our family again went to Korea for one and half years as for my father's Sabbatical after four years of missionary work. I was to be in fourth grade when I came back to Sierra Leone but I couldn't be a fourth grader because I forgot most of my English; I was put into the third grade.

The school that I attended was Lebanese International School. There were many kids there who teased me and my brothers whenever we spoke Korean. The attention made me want to get more and more of it, but also at the same time, I wanted to beat them up so they couldn't tease me anymore.

The first year in third grade was hard. I didn't understand what they were doing, so I had to study hard at home and memorize everything without understanding. After a year, I realized that in order to survive, I had to be a teacher's pet. So, I started studying like a mad cow running, and my toil gained its fruits. I suddenly became every teacher's favorite, and I had almost all the privileges that a student could ever want.

I could talk to my friends sometimes when they weren't allowed, I could drink water, I could talk with the teacher, which most students find hard to do, and so on. I was so proud of myself about achieving this goal that I became really arrogant. I found myself thinking I was better than all of my classmates. This was the main reason why I had only one true friend.

As I'm writing, I'm very ashamed of my past. I was a total jerk. Now, I can see that people did not want me to be arrogant but be a true, loyal friend; however, even if I had been such a friend, people would not have wanted to talk to me a lot because of my nerdy talk, at least that's what I think. Ninety-nine percent of my conversations with my friends were about homework and tests.

These experiences in Lebanese International School made me strong, and I developed the fortitude to tough out difficult situations. Even though this helped me a lot with social skills, it didn't do anything when it came to adjusting to Africa.

As a little girl, I was very ambitious. I wanted everything. Maybe this is the main reason why I hated and blamed my parents for choosing Africa as their missions field. I wanted the dresses or clothes and toys the Korean children had. The blaming continued until I don't know when.

I think that the day I stopped blaming my parents was the day I started taking responsibility. I started realizing that it was my responsibility to do what I thought was right, rather than trying to convince other people to do it. And that is also the same day I started opening my heart to Africa. There were several events that helped me adjust and understand Africa better, like I do now.

One of them is that whenever I tell people that I come from Africa, they would start by opening their mouth and widening their eyes. Then they would ask how I would live in such a place. It always makes me mad when this happens. I don't consider Africa as a bad place. Some people in Africa are happier than we are, who are not Africans. They try hard to earn money to feed their family. Their biggest goal is to eat three meals a day, and here we are, who have everything, complaining about stuff we don't have and use money to fill our greed.

These encounters made me think about how Africans are wonderful. It made me feel like I'm proud of being part or witnessing this life-struggle of Africans. Most people who come to Africa for short missions trip, sponsored by their church youth group, cry because they have everything and Africans don't. This is wrong, in my opinion; Africans aren't poor in the things that really matter. They have something we don't have. They have happiness. They can laugh out of something that is small or be happy about having something small.

I was very worried about hating Africa after I've been to the United States of America and Korea in later periods in my life; where we had all day electricity and all the supplies that were needed. I was worried about being my old selfish self again. I loved Africa with all my hearts, but it might have changed after experiencing comfort zone of Korea and the USA.

However, that was the stupidest thing I have done my life; worrying about my hating Africa, because as soon as stepped down the

115

stairs of the airplane, I felt like I came back home, that I finally came back where I belong. Africa is not just a place for me, it is the place where I grew up and where most of my memories are.

Africa is the place where I want to be. There might be some things needed, but this is the place where I want to devote my life to for the glory of the Triune God. This might be only for now, but I don't think I will ever want to change. The countries' boundaries and the languages are the only different things; if you go around Africa, Africans look alike and they live alike. The only problem is the language difference.

Right now, the feeling about me adjusting to Africa is only natural, only human, I guess. I just need to open my heart. I don't think I can live like Africans, completely, but I think I can talk with them or spend time with them. And I can come to understand them and their experience. If you get to know them, you would find out how wonderful they are. I just love Africa where I can be free of being myself. I have no pressure. I feel a belonging. I feel like I am a part of the land and the people.

Africa has given me a dream. My dream is to be a nurse or a doctor, who is trained by the best schools, who will come back to Africa and help the Africans. If my parents were not missionaries here, I would never have become adjusted to Africa and love it as my own. I thank God for sending my parents as missionaries of the Korean Presbyterian Church (Ko-Shin) denomination. Now, Africa is my hometown. It is the place where my precious memories have started.

About the Editor

Sora Yang is the 1st place winner of 2008 Rev. Ham Suk-Hyun Global Essay Contest, on the topic of "My Korean Identity." Sora is a junior at Baulkham Hills Selective High School in Sydney, Australia, which is a high school for academically gifted youth. Sora has won many important awards throughout her young life, such as Silver Duke of Edinburgh Award, Korean Consulate Award for Excellence in Korean, and 1st place in Japanese. Previously, in 8th grade, Sora won 3rd place in a state-wide essay competition of New South Wales Federation of Community Language Schools on the topic of "Why My Parents or Grandparents Chose Australia to be their Home." Sora Yang aspires to go to Harvard Law School and become a legal expert.

www.ingramcontent.com/pod-product-compliance
Lightning Source LLC
Chambersburg PA
CBHW061751270326
41928CB00011B/2457